Words of Wisdom

Words of Wisdom

A Compilation of Inspirational Messages

Sherry D. Bailey

authorHOUSE®

AuthorHouse™
1663 Liberty Drive
Bloomington, IN 47403
www.authorhouse.com
Phone: 1-800-839-8640

Scripture quotations marked NIV are taken from the Holy Bible, New
International Version®. NIV®. Copyright © 1973, 1978, 1984 by International
Bible Society. Used by permission of Zondervan. All rights reserved. [Biblica]

Published by AuthorHouse 02/20/2015

ISBN: 978-1-4969-1326-5 (sc)
ISBN: 978-1-4969-7231-6 (e)

Print information available on the last page.

Any people depicted in stock imagery provided by Thinkstock are models,
and such images are being used for illustrative purposes only.
Certain stock imagery © Thinkstock.

This book is printed on acid-free paper.

Contents

A Portrait of Praise

God is great! His greatness is not predicated on your goodness. No matter how good you live your life, it will never compare to God's greatness! In Malachi 3:6, it says, "I am the Lord, I do not change." But we do. We change our hair; we change our minds; we change where we work; where we go to school, and we change where we worship, amongst many things. Our God is a loving God. He is a merciful God. He wants His people to love, worship and bring glory and honor to Him. But do we? God said in the "b" section of Malachi 3:6, "so you descendants of Jacob are not consumed (or destroyed). God is telling us that He could take us out, but because His love is so vast, infinite, awesome, breath-taking, and everlasting that He chooses not to.

We can never compare to God's goodness. Our capacity for doing right cannot equal God's goodness. At best we can only bow down in awe and reverence to our Lord. I'm reminded of the story in Rev 4:6, where they are four living creatures in the center of the throne of God. The first living creature is like a lion, the second is like an ox; the third living creature is like a man; and the fourth living creature is like a flying eagle. Now I don't know why these four living creatures look like this, but I could imagine it takes the courage of a lion, the strength of an ox, the humanity of a man and the freedom of an eagle to recognize greatness. And to know "greatness" deserves praise, glory and honor.

As I was reading the book of Ezekiel I discovered the symbolism of the four living creatures. The Lion represents Jesus' kingship, the ox represents Jesus as Servant, the man represents Jesus' perfect humanity and the eagle represents Jesus' deity. Each of the four living creatures have six wings. And the six wings are covered with eyes all around them; even under their wings. Day and night they never stop saying, "Holy, holy, holy, is the Lord God Almighty, who was, and is, and is to come." Now while this is going on the 24 elders respond to the four living creatures by echoing God's praises. They declare, "You are worthy, our Lord and God, to receive glory and honor and power, for you created all things, and by your will, they were created and have their being." (Rev 4:11).

Now can you visualize this? Living creatures in heaven are having a praise party all day long. Guess what? It's not a quiet party. It's loud and boisterous. It is bursting with euphoria. It is rhythmic. It is on key. It is energetic. It is infectious and explosive! As children of God it should motivate us to give God glory in everything. Too often we become complacent, combative and critical of others, ourselves and the world. When we really just need to examine our ways and think about God's ways. I can assure you that you will not be able to remain in a somber and stagnant state visualizing the Lord of Host. The mere mention of his name should catapult you into praise. His name should propel you into action. His name should motivate you to give of yourself. There is no end to God's goodness. And when you think about that—you have to do as the elders did. You are compelled to say, "you are worthy our Lord to receive glory and honor and power." After all God says in His word, Psalm 8:4, "what is man that you are mindful of him, the son of man that you care for him? You were made a little lower than the heavenly beings and crowned him with glory and honor."

Now seeing that God has us on his mind when he created the world; why is it hard for us to break out in a praise? We know that we are "fearfully and wonderfully made" in his image, according to Psalm 139:14. We know that we are "more than conquerors" according to Roman 8:37. We know that we if we "humble ourselves God will exalt us" according to Luke 8:14. So tell me then how is it that we fail to give God glory? Considering he bestowed his glory on to us, why is so difficult to reciprocate? God has given us dominion. It says so in Psalm 8:6, "you made him to rule over the works of your hands, you put everything under his feet." And the last part of that chapter says, "O Lord, Our Lord, how majestic is your name in all the earth." So go ahead and praise him.

God's people were created to give God glory and honor. Let's draw a portrait of why, when and how you praise God. You can determine how you want your portrait to look. I want to share my portrait of praise. First of all, you have to ask yourself . . . Why do I praise God? The simple answer to why I praise God is because He deserves it. The intelligent answer is because he went to the Cross. Can you imagine what it was like back there in antiquity when Jesus was on the scene with his disciples? He came down from heaven to earth to save sinners like us. My Jesus walked up Golgotha's hill carrying a heavy cross, condemned by a pompous priest and religious leaders, but innocent of all charges. Our Lord and Savior went to the Cross in the midst slanderous insults; arrogant outsiders and silent followers. He was subjected to the brutal lashes of piercing whips, the rusty six-inch nails ripping his flesh open, the sinking, senseless thorns slicing his forehead and the ravishing spear piercing his side. Jesus suffered brutality. He suffered pain. He suffered inhumanity. And he did it all for your sake and mine. **Why** should I praise God? I praise Him because He is my Savior!

I praise God because he is the Alpha and Omega.
He is the creator.
He is the Lily of the Valley.
He is the Bright and Morning Star. I praise God because . . .
He is the Rose of Sharon.
He is the Great I Am.
He is a wheel in the middle of a wheel. I praise God because . . .
He never changes.
He is King of Kings.
He is a Mighty Counselor.
He is a Rock in a weary Land. I praise God because . . .
He is food on my table.
He is my company keeper.
He is my light. I praise God because . . .
He is a Heart-fixer.
He is my lawyer in a court room.
He is balm in Gilead.

He is mind regulator. I praise God because . . .

He is the Prince of Peace.

He is my Battle axe.

He is My Shepherd. I praise God because . . .

He is my all and all.

He is Lord!

He is merciful.

He is a Strong Tower. Why do I praise him?

I praise him because He is a Mighty God.

He is my Refuge.

He is my Strength.

He is the Rock of My Salvation. Why do I praise him?

I praise him because . . .

He is Lord of Lords.

He is water when I'm thirsty.

He is my Comforter.

He is my Healer. I praise him because . . .

He is Omnipotent (all-powerful).

He is Omniscient (all-knowing).

He is Omnipresent (everywhere at the same time).

I praise him because . . .

He is my Father when I'm fatherless.

He is my Mother when I'm motherless.

He is My Savior.

He is My Redeemer.

He is My God.

I've talked about why I praise God. And now I want to talk about **when** do you praise God? You praise God while you have breath. In the word of God the Psalmist wrote, "let everything that has breath praise the Lord." (Psalm 150:6). So when is it appropriate to praise God? Now! Now while the blood is still warm in your body. Now while you have eyes to see, lungs to breathe, ears to hear; a tongue to speak and hands to touch. Praise God now while he's here. Isaiah 55:6 says, "call on the Lord while he is near." Praise God now while he's keeping you. Praise God now while you have a chance. Praise God now because He's been so good. Praise God now because He deserves it. Praise God now because you are still here. Praise God now because He had mercy on you. Praise God now because he kept the death angel away. Praise God now because you're committed to serving him more. Praise God now because he died for your sins and mine. Praise God now because he set you free! Praise God now because you trust him. Praise God now because he loves you! Praise God now because he forgave your sins. Praise God now because He is your Savior!

I don't know about you, but if I had an opportunity to praise him I wouldn't let it pass me by. I'll praise him because He is good. I praise him because my thoughts are not his thoughts, nor are my ways his ways. (Isah 55:8). He has declared his glory into the heavens and the earth. He spoke existence into nothing and created man out of dust with his breath. If I were you I would praise God now because of who he is. I'm closing now. Before I go I have to tell you that as a child of the Most High God I can truly say that I am a PRAISER! And I pray that you are too. I pray that you give your God the praise that he deserves. I've talked about **why** we praise God and **when** to praise God, but now I have to tell you **how** to praise God. I want to suggest three ways to praise Him.

First you can praise him with your **hands**.
Secondly, you can praise him with your **feet**.
Thirdly, you can praise him with your **mouth**.

Let me call on three witnesses that can testify **how** they praised God. Look at the woman with the issue of blood. She used her hands, her feet and her mouth to give God the praise. Can you see her? There she is trapped in the crowd among hundreds of followers trying to see the Master. There she is in her loneliness, in her emptiness, in her broken-ness, and in her sickness . . . . bleeding for 12 long years without a ray of hope, but she heard Jesus was passing by. So she got the courage to press her way through the crowd, but how? She said, "I'll get down on my knees, I'll crawl on the ground, but I must see Jesus." She used her feet to press her way through the crowd, she used her hands to crawl to where Jesus was and she used her mouth to call upon the Lord. The woman with the issue of blood is a portrait of praise.

There's another woman. You know her. She's the woman at the well. Remember the sister with the attitude towards Jesus? She came to the well at hottest time of the day, probably around 12 noon, when she thought she wouldn't be harassed by the other women of the village. She came seeking water for herself; but she got so much more. This is a woman who was living with her man. She had been married five times before, but those marriages didn't work out. Jesus came to the well asking this sister for a drink. And how does she respond? Instead of giving him water, she asked him why are you asking me for a drink? Her response was, " . . . don't you know that I am a Samaritan and Jews don't associate with Samaritans?" Jesus calmly explained to her WHO HE is and why she should be asking him for "living water." After the final discourse the woman at the well was instantaneously transformed. She had to run (with her feet) and gesture I'm sure (with her hands) as well as shout (with her mouth) about the goodness of God. She ran back to her village telling her family and friends and all who would listen about a man name Jesus.

My final witness of **how** to praise God is a woman you remember well. She is the woman with the alabaster jar. As Jesus' death on the Cross was closely approaching the time came to prepare his body for burial. Preparation had to be made. And Mary was the woman with the alabaster jar who played a pivotal part in this process. Jesus was in a home eating dinner with his disciples and she came into the room. Mary was carrying a very expensive bottle of perfume. It equates to a year's worth of wages. As she sees her Lord and King reclined at the table, she approaches him with a steadfast and deliberate walk because she is on a mission. The only problem is that she is considered a loose woman. She doesn't travel in the status quo circles. She is a woman of the streets. She wears provocative clothing, flashy jewelry and vibrant colors on her face and fingers. She usually wears her hair long and carries a scarlet scarf around her neck. As she gets closer to Jesus she notices the disciple's disdain and disapproval, but she doesn't let that sway her. She continues to seek out her Master. As she gets closer to Jesus; she begins to fall to her knees, dropping to the ground in awe, she loses her own sandals in her anxiousness to get to Jesus, but she doesn't even notice. As she clutches the expensive perfume in her arms she begins to extend the alabaster jar towards Jesus. She opens the jar and an insatiable aroma of sunny blossoms, honey-suckle flowers and sweet smelling roses, chrysanthemums, lilies, carnations and orchids envelope the room. She pours the fragrance on Jesus' feet while kissing his precious toes. The oil spills onto his body. Undeniably this woman with the alabaster jar represents a portrait of praise. You see she praised God with her hands when she opened the alabaster jar. She praised God with her feet when she arrived in the room and bowed at Jesus' feet. And finally she praised God with her mouth when she kissed his precious feet. I don't know of a better portrait of praise than this one. This is an extraordinary example of how to praise God.

You see as children of God we should always praise him for **WHO** he is, **WHAT** he has done and **WHO** we are. My God is a good God. And I can't help but praise him. I hope your portrait is a vibrant as the one I have tried to paint for you today. No matter what your portrait displays make sure your portrait is full of praise.

Are You Thirsty?

In life we can all reminisce about going to a party. You can recall the energy and excitement you felt in anticipation of what was going to happen at the party. As you recall those memories of party life; I'm sure you can remember that they were naysayers, haters and celebrators at the party. It's similar to where we find our Savior Jesus Christ in the scripture we are preaching from today. (John 7:37).

It was the last day of the Feast of Tabernacles. It was a week-long celebration where the Israelites remember and celebrate how God had provided for them in the wilderness. They remembered how God allowed them to live in tents while delivering them from slavery. As you can imagine they were people everywhere. I'm sure they were children running and laughing. There was music playing. They were people singing, dancing and drinking. And I'm sure somebody was barbequing. You could smell the meat cooking; hear the animals squawking; hear the wheels of the chariot trampling under the dirt, hear the sound of drums; the merriment of people carousing; drunks murmuring and girls giggling. The scene is similar to what Black folks would say is a family reunion in the Summertime. In the midst of celebration we have Jesus who has just taught in the Temple standing and making a statement. He proclaimed his prophetic purpose to the people.

Isn't life profound? Imagine if you will, you are at a party. What would you think if while you're trying to get your groove on; your drink on; or your grind on—that the Master of the Universe steps on the scene and speaks to the core of your heart? He speaks to that insatiable hunger and thirst in your heart that you thought was dead. He speaks to your inner man—your spirit man. You try to ignore him, but you can't. You try to pretend like you can't hear him, but you can. You can't help it because you know there is something missing in your life. You are in a dry season. You are suffering from spiritual desiccation. In other words, you are suffering from spiritual dryness. You're completely dry. You're void of power. Not only are you suffering from spiritual desiccation; but you are suffering from spiritual impudence. You are powerless and ineffective. The worst part is you know it. And you haven't done anything. Truth is you haven't heard a word to soothe your dry decaying bones in a while. Life's struggles have left you destitute, desolate and despondent. You are in a dry season impoverished by your own circumstances. The dirt of the world has stripped you of effectiveness; but like all party-goers you desire to have fun. You long for your drought season to be quenched. The question is—Are you thirsty? I know you are, but how do you quench your thirst?

I want to submit to you how you can get not just any water; but living water! The first thing you must do to get living water is: 1) you must **come** to Jesus. That is our first point. We must come to Jesus. I didn't say come to church—your presence today attests to the fact you come to church, but God desires for you to come to Christ.

Many of us don't want to come because we are more comfortable with "going." We are familiar with the passage, "go make disciples," but not many of us are willing to "come" to Christ. We deceive ourselves by saying were working for the Lord in the name of "ministry" but Jesus is inviting you to come sit at his feet. He wants you to be still and draw closer to him. What happens with Church-goers is that we'll sit close to the fountain—but never drink. We won't even take a sip of the water the preacher is pouring. Instead we'll wave it away in disgust asserting that is for those other folks; when in actuality we are the ones dying of dryness. You're on a collision course; a destiny with death; but only if you remain there. John 7:37 says, "if you are thirsty come to me and drink."

The sad truth is life has infected you with deadness. You may be in a dead-end job, a dead-end relationship or a dead season, whatever the case you must admit that you are thirsty. The dirt of the world has infested you with pollution. The dirt of lying, the dirt of cheating, the dirt of back-biting, greed and envy has left you empty, dry and arid. I submit to you today the solution for your pollution is dilution. The dilution is Jesus Christ; the living water. He is waiting for you. Don't try to fix yourself up; don't try to clean yourself up—just come.

We should come to Jesus because we are thirsty for something. Some of us are thirsty for higher learning. We thirst for a nice or nicer home; a better vehicle; or a higher position, more money or for a better relationship. We all thirst for something. We should come to Jesus because He is the living water.

What I have discovered in God's word is that when Jesus invites you to "come" it's always packaged with a promise. Take Mark 11:28, When Jesus invites you to "come;" the promise of coming is "rest." Take John 3:36, when Jesus invites you to "come;" the promise is "everlasting life." Take Luke 18:16, when Jesus invites you to "come;" the promise is "the kingdom of God." Take John 4:14 it states, "whoever drinks the water I give him will never thirst." Indeed the water I give him will become like springs of water welling up to eternal life." That's a promise!

I've realized in my own life when I don't come to Christ of the scriptures it's because I'm experiencing spiritual dehydration or spiritual desiccation. Honestly, God invites you to come be with him every day, but we allow our agendas to get in the way. Every morning you wake up that's an invitation from Jesus. He is inviting you to come sit at his feet and learn more about him. When Jesus says "come" three (3) things are happening:

1. Invitation—Jesus is inviting you to be with Him
2. Participation—you must act to receive
3. Expectation—you expect to receive something

As celebrators (not haters) we do come to get something, right? The invitation wasn't only to drink—it was to be in covenant relationship with the Master. Without the relationship you cannot receive the promise. Remember I said when Jesus says, "come" it's always packaged with a promise. The promise is a free gift from God. And when you accept the invitation you receive the free gift. As believers all we have to do is take it. It is bestowed on to us (Exod 17:6). And when you drink from God's fountain you receive "grace;" "abundance" and "intimacy" with the Father.

When Jesus told Jonah to come to Nineveh it was not just a command; it was an invitation that required his participation. And I am sure he was expecting something to happen when he got there. The promise was that 120 thousand Ninevites were spared from destruction. It was the greatest revival in history. (Jonah 3:10). You may want to read that again. When Jesus says, "come" that should get your attention. Remember it's an invitation; it requires your participation and you have a sense of expectation. It carries with it an inherent expectation to receive something.

The second point I want to share is that you must "**believe**" in Jesus to get living water. You must believe in Jesus to get your drink on. As celebrators—lovers of Jesus, we must believe in order to receive. John 7:38 says, "whoever believes in me, as the scripture says, "streams of living water will flow from within him." When you believe in Jesus you possess eternal life. All you have to do is come, believe and receive. And why should you believe in Jesus? We should believe in Jesus because if you don't; you will die in your sins. (John 8:24). Believing in Jesus sets you free (John 8:31-32).

- 2 Cor 3:17 says, "*the Lord is the Spirit; and where the Spirit is there is freedom."*

- John 4:24 says, *"God is Spirit and his worshipers must worship in spirit and in truth."*
- John 8:44 says, *"Those who do not believe belong to the devil."*

Are you a hater or a celebrator? If you are a part of the fellowship of celebrators you believe. You hear from God; you know God and he knows you. John 8:47 says children of God hear from God. As celebrators of Christ we thirst for him as a deer pants for water. (Psalms 44:1). We know we must believe to receive the living water. John 7, verse 38 says, "whomsoever believes in me, as the scripture says, "streams of living water will flow from within him."

If the disciples had a problem with believing you know you and I do at times. Jesus' brothers didn't believe who he was until they saw with their own eyes his miracles. When the disciples asked Jesus what must they do to do the work of God, he answered and said, "the work of the Lord is this: to believe in the one he has sent." (John 6:29). God said in his word, Heb 11:4, "He is a rewarder of them who diligently seek him." If you believe you're going to seek him; if you seek him you desire living water.

Living water is the catalyst. It's our life-line. It is our blood bought right; our enabler; our liberator; and our power source. Living water is your peace-maker; your heart regulator; your storm ceasor; your heavy-load sharer; your proclaimer and your intimate friend.

- God is the originator of living water.

- Jesus is the possessor of living water.
- The Holy Spirit is the manifestor of living water.

You cannot receive living water without going through the Son. John 14:6 says, "no one comes to the Father, except through the Son." You must go through Jesus to get the living water. If living water was the UT Football stadium you have to go through the gate to get it. If living water was the White House you have to go through the gate to get it. If living water was the Queen of England's palace you still have to go through the gate to get it. But living water is not any of those things. It's not from man—it's from God. The only way to get it—is to believe in the Son. Jesus said when you come and believe in him; you will never be thirsty. (John 6:35).

We need to approach the bible as the unadulterated, awesome and amazing truth of God. The bible is not a book to be read. It's our basic instruction manual before leaving earth. And until we begin to believe it, we won't receive or achieve all that God has for us. In effect, we will merely be party nay-sayers or by-standers who go to church, but never come to Christ. God's word is nothing to a believer or a saint if he doesn't believe it. We must believe. John 3:36 says, "whoever believes in the Son has eternal life, but whoever rejects the Son will not see life for God's wrath remains on him." As sinners we are guilty of sin, but God purges us from guilt by his precious blood. As saints we get dirty everyday that defiles us. That's why we need washing in the water of God's word to be cleaned.

Living water washes away every attack, every plot, and any virus that tries to attach itself to us. And thank God for Jesus because he is our living water that vaporizes the dirt. I'm sure some of you are familiar with computers. Most computers have an anti blocker on them to protect against unwanted junk mail. That's what Jesus does with our sin. The living water is Jesus' memory disk cleaner and he takes away the dirt and grime of the world and wipes it away with his spiritual antiseptic. It's called the blood of the Lamb. Our guilt keeps us in bondage, but Jesus is our guilt blocker because he is our living water. Because Jesus shed his precious blood on the Cross we have been exonerated. What the water can't clean the blood erases. It disintegrates and demolishes every stronghold. The blood and water have to exist for us to be victorious!

Finally, if you are thirsty you must **come** to Jesus; you must **believe** in Jesus and our third point is: we must **receive** Jesus to get living water. Remember earlier I told you each time Jesus says "come" in the bible it is packaged with a promise. Receiving is no different. Jesus said when you come to him you receive. Amazing! We receive when we come to Jesus.

Do you want to come? Are you thirsty? Jesus spoke in a loud voice at the Feast of Tabernacles. He said if anyone is thirsty let him come. The invitation has been extended will you respond? When you're defiled by the world you need to get clean by washing in the Word of God. You pick up dirt from people and you pick up dirt from life's circumstances. The only real cure for defilement is water. Washing in the water through the Word is the solution for your pollution. Christ loved us so much that he gave himself up for us through the blood and the water. The blood redeemed us and the water cleanses us.

- The blood purges; the water sanctifies;
- The blood sets us free, the water ushers us to freedom;
- The blood bonds us to the Son; the water connects us to the Spirit;
- The blood boasts of His goodness; the water symbolizes his mercy;
- The blood takes away every tear and pain; the water extinguishes sins' stain;
- The blood captures the scene at the Cross; the water pours out so that none will be lost;
- The blood snatches the keys from hell and exonerates; the water carries you to Heaven's gate;

You have an insatiable thirst that can only be satisfied with living water. Receiving living water is not just physical; but it has to be mental as well. Even though we may all be in the church it doesn't mean we receive the Word that is being shared. It is like an empty pitcher. It can only receive whatever you put in it; but if it's not in the right position to receive; the pitcher's purpose is ineffective. If the pitcher is upside down or turn to its side it cannot receive the water you're putting in it. It's like us—if we come into the church with our minds on everything but God; we won't receive the Word God has for us. Jeremiah said it like this, you have committed two sins against God: 1) rejected the Son which is the living water; and 2) you have dug for yourself empty cisterns that cannot hold water. (Jer 2:13b).

Digging empty cisterns is like being preoccupied with the things of the world. It detracts your focus from the things of God.

Church goers come to church; but they don't receive the living water because their mind is not on God. They have a different agenda. They come to transact business; catch up on the latest gossip; come to mack a mate for their next rendezvous or simply come to "play church." That is what I mean when I say "receiving is mental." If you're not in the right position—mentally you can't receive. When Jeremiah said, "you have dug your own cisterns"—he was talking about containers that hold water. Church goers come to church with empty and corrupted minds and polluted temples and think their physical presence will get them into Heaven. What a mistake! We as believers should know that the only way to Heaven is by believing and confessing the Lord Jesus as our Savior. (Rom 10:9). We must be in the right position to receive the living water. Then we will be victorious. And God's glory can be manifested in our lives.

Satisfy your thirst with the Word of God. He will wet your mouth with living water. You will thirst no more. Come saints, come sinners, whosoever will, let him come and be satisfied by the rivers of living water. Christ has paid the ultimate price for our sins. Give him your life and watch him fill you with overflowing love and forgiveness. Remember when you're thirsty all you have to do is come, believe and receive. He's waiting for you.

Beauty for Ashes

$\mathscr{H}$ave you ever felt that you are a diamond in the rough, scattered beneath the dirt, filth and soot of your tumultuous past? Beneath the debris of your forgotten childhood; abandoned in the dirt of your scarred memories is a precious stone waiting to be discovered. Many of us have felt that. And I can attest that I was there once. Well, I'm not anymore. And I'm here to tell you that your beauty will emerge when you allow God to remove the ash of your past. God will reveal your beauty. Your beauty is in him.

Psalm 50:2 says, "from Zion, perfect in beauty God shines through." God wants to shine through you. First, we must repent because God demands it. Jeremiah speaks about repentance in the third chapter when he compares an unfaithful wife to unfaithful people. Each time Jeremiah says, "return" you could substitute the word "repent" in its place. As a matter of fact, God says if you only return (repent) "I will not be angry forever." (Jer 3:12). He says, "I will treat you like sons and give you a desirable land, the most beautiful inheritance of any nation." (Jer 3:19). WOW! God really desires for us to acknowledge that we need him. And we need God to forgive us and have mercy on our sin. I believe God wants to give you beauty for ashes. So let's look at how we can have that.

Isaiah 4:1-6 states, "seven women will take hold of one man." Seven represents completion (Exodus 20:10). God ordained the seventh day (Sunday) as a day of rest because he completed speaking the world into existence in six days. He rested on the 7th because he had completed his work. Seven also represents fulfillment. (Joshua 6:4). Joshua fulfilled God's command by marching around the walls of Jericho seven times on the seventh day with seven priest blowing seven trumpets. Joshua fulfilled his duty. And seven represents perfection (Revelations 1:4). John spoke to the seven churches through the Holy Spirit. He spoke about 7 bowls, 7 seals, 7 judgments and 7 new things. Everything God does is perfect. He is righteous perfection. And the bible tells us that even though we may fall seven times; {or more} the Lord will pick us up (Proverbs 24:16) again. Praise God!

Why will seven women take hold of one man? I don't know, but I think I may have a possible answer. Since seven represents completion, perfection and fulfillment it stands to reason that a man cannot do anything well without a woman. Gotcha. Made you laugh. But seriously, I think it takes spiritual fortitude of perfection, completion and fulfillment for us to see and realize what God has in store for us. And there are five phrases I want to lift up out of this text. According to the first phrase in this scripture it says, "take hold." I believe God wants us to "take hold" of His word in our everyday life. He wants us to be the "brilliant diamond" he created. When you really get it down in your Spirit WHO you are and WHY you were created—you can walk into this new place.

Isaiah 43:7 says you were created to glorify him. How do you that? You do that by "how" well you know your Father. The truth is the more you know about God the more beautiful you are. You got to take hold of him. Take hold of him like gum on the roof of your mouth. Take hold of Jesus like he took hold of you. He wants you to know that he is your Jehovah Sabaoath. That means "the Lord Almighty." It means the Lord of Hosts will fulfill his purpose even when we—his heavenly creatures fail. Try to visualize the host of heaven grasping you in the bosom of his arms. Visualize him standing with the Father and the Holy Spirit hovering overhead. Visualize the power of the God-head Trinity enveloping you. Visualize his peace, his presence and his power all wrapped around you. That's what you need to take hold of. The storms of life can be raging, but the Lord of the Armies has a grip on you. He won't let you fall into disaster. He will take hold of you. That grip is so tight that it can't be penetrated. It is the connectivity of your relationship with your Daddy that allows you to know in your gut that nothing can separate you from his love. Nothing can separate you from your birthright. It's an assurance that you know that you know who you are and whose you are. It's time to awake and see through the eyes of the King of Kings.

The second phrase I want to lift up is "be called." It says, the "daughters of Zion desire to **be called** by the Lord." Isn't that what you and I want? We want to be called a child of the King. That is the greatest honor. In reality, you know we are all his children; his daughter; his son—so why don't we act like it? It is because you've been called by so many names that you've forgotten who you really are. The lesson for us is that we should affirm our identity. In other words, we need to be whole and walk in authority; recognizing who we are. I learned another name God calls himself. It's Jehovah Muy-kay-dish-kim. It means "the Lord our Sanctifier." Isn't that awesome? To be called of God is the greatest calling. Even God called himself by name to affirm himself. And we have been called to.

Jeremiah said it in 1:5; like this, "before the foundations were formed I knew you." Before you were born he set you apart. That's incredible. God is saying before he spoke the world into existence you were a sparkle in his eye. He called you by name. Hallelujah! So affirm your identity. It's okay. God did. So can you. Isaiah 43:1,7 says, "he summoned you by name. He said, "you are mine." Men and women of God you've been called by the Lord of hosts to declare his praises. You are precious and honored in his sight. He loves you. You were called to declare his goodness and to be his witnesses. I just have one question. What are you waiting for? We have all been called according to Jeremiah and Isaiah. So start acting like it. And begin to affirm yourself.

The third phrase I want to lift up is "take away our disgrace." What's that? You know what it is. It is sin. It is the veil of self-degradation we succumb to when we don't realize our own value and potential. It's the veil of not seeing ourselves as we really are. God said he will remove the veil of fear and rejection. God will take away our disgrace. He will replace ash with grace. He will crown you with jewels and present you as his royalty! In order to do that it's important that we wash in the word daily. Washing implies cleansing. And cleanliness is next to godliness. If you want different results try doing something different. How about washing in the Word of God daily and allowing God to reveal his beauty for you. God says in Isaiah 54:4-8 he will reveal your beauty when your perspective shifts from self to Him.

The problem with a diamond is that it cannot see its' own reflection. I'm sure if we saw ourselves through God's eyes we would be amazed at our own beauty. God said he will take away the filth of the women of Zion. The truth is the more we know about God the more beautiful we are. There's a poem entitled, "Our Deepest Fear" I want to share. The words speak volumes. The author is Marianne Williamson.

"Our deepest fear is not that we are inadequate. Our deepest fear is that we are powerful beyond measure. It is our light, not our darkness, that most frightens us.

We ask ourselves, who am I not to be brilliant, gorgeous, talented and fabulous? Actually who are we not to be? You are a child of God. Your playing small does not serve the world. There's nothing enlightened about shrinking so that other people won't feel insecure around you.

We are all meant to shine, as children do. We were born to make manifest the glory of God that is within us. It's not just in some of us; it's in everyone. And as we let our own light shine, we unconsciously give other people permission to do the same. As we're liberated from our fear, our presence automatically liberates others."

So remember whose you are. Remember God has set you up to brag on his child. Let him have his way! God wants to take away your disgrace and put you in a high place. He wants to restore you so that you can walk into your new assignment.

The fourth phrase I want to lift up from the text is: "the Lord will wash away the filth of the daughters of Zion." As a diamond in the rough, I know you've been dumped on all your life, but you got to know that the Lord has decreed your sanctification! You've been washed clean by the blood of the lamb. Zechariah 9:16 states, "the Lord God will save you on that day. You will be a sparkle in the land; a jewel in his crown." Who can render a charge against you? I know the word of God. And it says when God acts who can reverse it? (Isaiah 43:13). Stop filling your head with Satan's filthy lies. Lamentations 3:37 says, "who can speak and have it happen if the Lord has not decreed it?" The Lord has called you by name and he has sanctified you. The Lord will wash away your sin. It is the Lord who is our sanitizer.

I wash my face in the morning when I wake up. I wash my car when it's dirt. I wash my hair when it needs it. But I know when I really want to get clean; I need to wash in the word of God. As Ephesians 5:26 says, "Jesus Christ, gave himself up for us to make us holy, by cleansing us with the Word of God." We are sanctified because his blood was shed on Calvery's Cross. He did that so that he could present us to himself without blemish and with flawless perfection. The only ONE who can make us WHOLE is the Lord. We can walk in boldness and confidence because the Lord has cleansed us from all sin. And he has washed away our filth.

Somebody needs to declare a word. Affirm yourself. I hear the Word of God say, "In God, whose word I praise, in God I trust; I will not be afraid. What can mortal man do to me?" (Psalm 56:11). Even though people can be plotting your demise God will protect. He said in Psalm 56:5, "all day long they twist my words . . . but Isaiah 57:6b says, "the pit they dug for me they will fall into." Hallelujah! God is righteous! He will not allow your enemies to hurt you.

The fifth phrase I want to lift up from the text is "a hiding place." God says he will be our shelter and shade from the storm and rain. Everyone at some point in life wants to get away. We all need to get away from the hustle and bustle of life. How many times can you recall thinking of a place of refuge? How many times do you think of a hiding place? I am sure it was too numerous to mention. But no matter how many times you thought of it—you probably were not able to get away right then. However, God is saying he is your "hiding place." Whenever you feel lonely, whenever you feel in despair or disgraced Jesus said, "come unto me all who are weary and heavy laden and I will give you rest." (Matt 11:28). He is our hiding place. He will satisfy all our needs. He is the only a thought away. And he is as close as a whisper. Your hiding place doesn't always have to be physical. It can be mental. It is an attitude of quietness and peace. Your hiding place can be as natural as breathing. Try exhaling negative thoughts and inhaling the word of God. Do that and watch your vision become clearer.

My final point is that we must reside in his presence. When you do that God says the dirt of your life will disintegrate. And your God-given beauty will emerge. He said in Psalm 91:1-2, "he who dwells in the shelter of the Most High, will rest in the shadows of the Almighty. I will say to the Lord, He is my refugee and my fortress, my God, in whom I trust." Just as God has promised; he is more than able to fulfill his purposes. His word will accomplish what he intended. He wants you to know that you are the righteousness of God. You are the glory and splendor of his majesty! You are cedars of Lebanon. You are the righteous branch of Israel. It would do us well to recognize and recall what David said in Psalm 84:11-12, "for the Lord God is a sun and shield; the Lord bestows favor and honor, no good thing does he withhold from those whose walk is blameless." God is our shield and our fortress; he will give you favor and honor when you walk according to his way.

Finally, remember God is saying, "lift up your heads, oh ye gates and be ye lifted up ye everlasting doors and the King of glory shall come in. Who is the King of glory? The Lord is strong and mighty. The Lord is mighty in battle. He is the King of glory. (Psalm 24:7-10). Affirm, wash and reside in God. He will remove the ash of guilt and shame and give you beauty. And he will call you by your name. We are his. Give your ash to God. And he will grant you grace.

African Theology

There is a common faulty assumption that African theology is an archaic, uncivilized and impudent religion. I disagree with this notion and will ambitiously attempt to argue the contrary. After having read Bediako's book, "African Theology" I am enlightened, empowered and enraged by the Europeans ideology of the subject. I believe it is the unconscious and grossly inaccurate misperception of the European to consider "African theology" a religion for the barbaric and the uneducated, according to one theologian. However, as history has taught us "African theology" has its roots in the biblical cannon as attested in Genesis 12:2, *"I will make you into a great nation and I will bless you, I will make your name great, and you will be a blessing."* We are the seed of Abraham therefore co-heirs according to the promise. Respectively, Galatians 3:28-29 states, *"There is neither Jew or Greek, slave or free, male or female, for you are all one in Christ Jesus. If you belong to Christ then you are Abraham's seed, and co-heirs according to the promise."* African Americans have been demoralized, degraded and debilitated by Europeans since the inception of slavery thus being relegated to the bottom of the scale as viewed by theologian, Robert July. Additionally, West-Indian theologian Edward Blyden stated Christianity endorsed slavery is to "induce the Negro into submissiveness;" whereas, Westerners capitalized, I believed. As an African American I know all too well the ramifications of oppression by the European.

I will assert that African theology has three unifying elements which make it a powerful shift in the center of gravity of Christianity. Those watershed elements are indigenization; translatability and liberation.

African theology is the art of indigenization and ethnocentricity. The premise of indigenization is the supposition that Christ accepts us as we are. Indigenization is defined as how we express ourselves in the world. With that in mind, it would seem reasonable to conclude that African theology for the African is replete with an inferiority complex that has resulted in the inculturation of the African, at the hands of so-called "Christian missionaries." It was the intent of the western missionary to bring Christianity to the continent of Africa thus "civilizing" a savage race of people; however that mission was predicated and built upon fallacy and fortune. Indigenization implies being true to one's culture. Inculturation ushered in new theology, customs and tradition leaving the African perplexed about his own self-worth and self-identity. The African's self-identity is a stake when a foreigner comes into his country and subjugates him into accepting their "Christian customs" while devaluing the African's customs, faith and tradition, resulting in the African's viewpoint of his theology to be irrelevant or inconsequential; and the Westerner's Christianity as superior and therefore right. We must see that there are systematic, institutionalized and discriminatory practices at work. And they are deteriorating the core of the African people.

Ethnocentricity is a luxury of self-appreciation and self-understanding for the African. In 1971, Osofo Damauh delved into African traditional religion and proposed there were four contending forces for the African: 1) traditional religion; 2) Christianity; 3) Islam and 4) religious identity by indifferent materialism. Damuah argued Africans viewed Christianity as "a white man's religion" because Europeans diminished the African culture. I agree with Damuah. It is because of that submission to Christianity that African Americans are struggling with their own identity today in America. Self-hate, assimilation and degradation come to mind when viewed in the context of how some African Americans treat each other in relation to the European. Credit can also be attributed to Willie Lynch for leaving an indelible mark on the African for their self-hate. He was the founder, father and originator of slavery submission. He left a legacy of pitting the slave against one another while diametrically devaluing his intellect but preserving his body. This mantra was extremely successful and still continues today.

Assimilation is an everyday and normal practice for the African American when he or she looks in the mirror. Ordinarily they don't see beauty rather brutality; therefore they painstakingly exhaust all financial resources to "assimilate" to the European culture for acceptance. A great number of them buy homes they can't afford; buy vehicles they cannot insure let alone maintain and straighten their kinky hair to look like the White woman. They adorn themselves to look more like the White man. They send their children to all white schools to educate them so they can compete and articulate like the

White race. Self-understanding and appreciation appear to be an allusive quality that is slipping through the fingers of the African American. It appears too fleeting for them to grasp.

Ethnocentricity has seemingly deteriorated in the African American culture as well. Degradation is the number one order of the day in relation to black on black behavior. It is a common practice for African American males to call each other "dawg" or "Niggah." Similarly some African American females adopt this same practice by calling each other "bitch" or "whore." These senseless acts are seen as reprehensible and repugnant by any other race, but not so for African Americans. There is no need to solicit help from "the man" to keep them disenfranchised; they do that proudly and willingly without a second thought. I am deeply inflamed with this injurious and asinine mentality. It corrodes our culture and disfigures our faces assigning our destiny to a self-induced and disastrous doom. In the 1970's black pride was at an all time high. African Americans would take to the streets espousing "black power" while lifting their right arm and clutching their fist as a symbol of solidarity to their culture. So much has changed since then. Today the African American is at odds with himself (self-degradation) or at odds with his brother (dissention) and spiritually at odds with his faith (moral disentegration).

I believe the righteous path to our African theology is the power to be one's self and still be true to his or her faith. In other words, as an African American woman I should take pride in my blackness, even though I am of a lighter hue than many of my counterpart sisters. And I should embrace my Nubian features without experiencing some identity crisis by seeking ways to assimilate to my White sister's culture. I must conceive and believe the truth—that I am Black and beautiful and therefore I will not be threatened by a sense of impiousness to my self-identity.

One of African theology's greatest goals is to execute translatability. We, as Christians can espouse all the rhetoric we want about carrying out our duty; but without repeated tangible examples of actualizing the message of Jesus Christ we fail miserably. As Mbiti states, "we can add nothing to the Gospel, for this is an eternal gift of God, but Christianity is always a beggar seeking food and drink, cover and shelter from the cultures it encounters in its never-ending journeys and wanderings." Mbiti further states the purpose of translatability, "we cannot artificially create an "African theology" or even plan it; it must evolve spontaneously as the Church teaches and lives her faith and in response to the extremely complex situation in Africa. One cannot ignore that indigenization, translatability and incarnation are synonymous with universality. And these concepts belong on a continuum and are integral to the warp and woof of the Christian religion," as Bediako states. What I find most intriguing is the notion of translatability by Mbiti as he answers the question of its validity. He persuades the reader by stating, "God, the Father of our Lord Jesus Christ is the same God who has been known and worshipped in various ways within the religious life of African peoples' and who therefore, was "not a stranger in Africa prior to the coming of missionaries." They did not bring God; rather God brought them, so that by the proclamation of the Gospel through the missionary activity, Jesus Christ might be known, for "without Him (Jesus Christ) the meaning of our religiosity is incomplete." I believe that is an excellent point. In my opinion, it means the White man cannot claim to have "enlightened" the Black man through his Western religion. On the contrary, it was God who should be credited. Furthermore, as a Black people we know who we are and no other culture can thwart our identity. And James reaffirms Bediako's belief saying true religion is, "to *look after the orphans and widows in their distress and to keep oneself from being polluted by the world."* (1:27). Accordingly, Matthew's gospel points out, "*I tell you the truth, whatever you did for one of the least of these brothers of mine, you did for me."* (25:30).

While I must admit the burden of actualizing translatability in my own life can be somewhat problematic at this time, but I still must rise to the occasion. Consequently, on any given day; I can see myself proudly praying for the sick, helping the needy and dispersing food to the hungry. I would like to think that I am a good Christian who "walks the walk and does not just talks the talk;" but that is not the truth. Sure in theory it is; but not in practicality. As an abused wife, separated from her pastor husband and raising a five year-old son alone with very little financial and emotional support etc; I find it an onerous task to carry out the gospel message at this point in my journey. I am suffering from major depressive disorder with homicidal ideations and self-destructive tendencies while functioning as a mother, student and Christian. However, the rest of my story has yet to be told.

My present personal theology is to help those who are hemorrhaging in life; especially those who desire to have a better life. Don't get me wrong I am not espousing to indiscriminately insist on being the judge of who is worthy or unworthy to receive blessings; what I am postulating is that those members in our churches, our places of abode, our communities those who we are hurting—whether physical, psychological and/or spiritual; we should stretch out our hand to assist them. I cannot count the number of times I personally have been in need, whether it was for food, gas in my vehicle or for someone to be a handyman and fix something in my quaint apartment; that I did not reach out to inquire for help. Why—because I am not in fellowship or relationship with my so-called church. Rather I rely on the good intentions and charity of my seminary community. Translatability for me is maintaining my personal Christianity while being immersed in a predominately Presbyterian community. It is one that I know very little about. I need to connect with while at the same time needing to maintain my own African American identity. Should I reach out more to my fellow students? Yes of course, but when was the last time you witnessed a sick, depraved and mentally challenged person seek company and intellectual dialogue? On the contrary, he or she would prefer to stand alone and find comfort in the solace of his/her isolation. I admire the way Langston Hughes spoke of ethnocentricity. He said, " . . . *I am the darker brother. They send me to eat in the kitchen when company comes, but I laugh, and eat well, and grow strong. Tomorrow I'll be at the table when company comes. Nobody we'll dare say to me "eat in the kitchen, then. Besides, they'll see how beautiful I am. And be ashamed. I to, am America."*

The words of this poem reiterate my portrayal of how I see myself, my theology and my community. I maybe hemorrhaging but I be damned if I am going to let the powers that be hold me down. I am resilient, strong and courageous. I translate my theology by waking up every morning and resolving to keep going.

My final argument in investigating and identifying the unifying elements in African theology is to state that it is one of liberation and pilgrimage. The meaning of liberation in this vein illustrates the redemption of the African culture. Has the Black man redeemed himself now that we have a Black president? That is a question only he can answer. I believe African theology is the power, the privilege and the personal responsibility of Africans and African-Americans to demand, to insist and assert their God-given right to demand justice. We must encourage, identify and if need be forcibly call for liberation from oppressors, liberation from politics that institutionalize and demoralize us; and liberation from the tyranny of degradation. We, as African Americans must expect, employ and investigate the truth of our heritage. We must unashamedly delve into our ancestry and gain knowledge, wisdom and discernment from our deceased relatives; so that we can justly actuate our faith in the future. It is incumbent upon us as a people to perpetuate our culture, dig into our heritage and celebrate our lineage; so that our children's children and their off-spring can strongly and unswervingly take a place at the table—the table of equality, democracy and peace.

We need to liberate ourselves from our own faulty misperception and idiosyncrasies that we are inept or inferior. Instead, we should bravely enter into a new paradigm shift of hope and promise. We need to acquire possession of the American dream while simultaneously sharing it with our brother and sister. I believe our liberation and pilgrimage defines us as a nation. It equates us as God's children thus leveling the playing field and uniting us as one body of Christ. The bible says, "he who believes in the Father will have everlasting life." (John 3:16). We are united by the father therefore we should accept our common destiny. By believing our heritage we know our pilgrimage is taking us to the same place.

The unifying element that bonds us together is *belief* or *faith* in Christ Jesus. Our struggle to make sense of our world, to empathize or understand our neighbor whose is of a different culture is an arduous task I admit, but it is doable. When we determine in our mind to resolve to work out our own salvation with fear and trembling; then we can conquer our fears and sit at the table together in dignity and not like savages. Our impiousness for one another stifles and incapacitates us to the point where it strips us of even the semblance of liberation. When our forefathers involuntarily made their pilgrimage to America, Christianity was forced upon him; he was beaten into submission; ripped of his manhood/womanhood; while being denied the right to celebrate his ethnocentricity. The doctrine of inculturation was the first order of business along with that of indentured servitude. Engelbert Mveng, a Cameroonian theologian gives attention to the impoverished state of the African and states, "poverty on a material level takes in account the exploitation and suffering of African people who have as experience been the most humiliated people in history in their social and cultural identity as well as their humanity."

I submit a most grievous error in America has been wrought. It was an error that was not derived from the African—rather it was spearheaded by the Westerner leaving the African as a merciless victim. It has been a diabolical nightmare whereas the African has been unable to awaken from. We must see our pilgrimage as our own declaration of independence, our emancipation proclamation, our Manifesto and personal theology to proclaim a bright future that is "so wondrously clear." We must declare our freedom despite the dissenting odds, as Maya Angelou describes in her poem, "Still I Rise," *you may write me down in history with your bitter twisted lies, but like dust, still I rise.*" We must hear the voices of our ancestors in their native tongue as they cry and plead for our appeal. We must listen and implement their hopes and dreams of a better quality of life. With that same synergy we can burst into jubilation exclaiming the atrocities have been annihilated and the demons have been destroyed. They have all been slain by the blood of the Lamb. It is then when we can see liberation be realized. It is not a dream deferred, but an imminent watershed of reality that we can all share. As the African theology premise postulates; "true power and authority is not at all in a man; instead it comes from (ancestors)—one who sits on the stool of the ancestors." And if one were to discount the traditional rule of African theology it would be "undermining the very foundations of the identity and continuity of the state or community itself," as Meyer Fortes and Evans-Prichard attests.

In conclusion, my concept of African theology is ingrained in the seven principles of Kwanzaa—an African agriculture celebration called the "first fruits." The seven principles are rooted in a common set of values and practices that are germane to Africa; ingathering; reverence; commemoration; recommitment and celebration. Kwanzaa principles are: "<u>Umoja</u> meaning unity; and to strive for and maintain unity in the family, community, nation and race; <u>Kujichagulia</u> meaning self-determination; to define ourselves, name ourselves, create for ourselves and speak for ourselves instead of being defined, named, created for and spoken for by others; <u>Ujima</u> meaning collective work and responsibility; which is to build and maintain our community together and make our sister's and brother's problems our problems and to solve them together; <u>Ujamaa</u> meaning Cooperative Economics; to build and maintain our own stores, shops and other businesses and to profit from them together; <u>Nia</u> meaning purpose: it is to make our collective vocation the building and developing of our community in order to restore our people to their traditional greatness; <u>Kuumba</u> meaning Creativity; which is to do always as much as we can in the way we can, to leave our community more beautiful and beneficial than we inherited it; and finally <u>Imani</u> meaning Faith; which is to believe with all our heart in our people, our parents, our teachers, our leaders and the righteousness and victory of our struggle," as espoused by Maulana Karenga. My African theology is to practice these seven principles daily. I actualize these principles by being dutiful to my community in spending my money locally. I do that by sharing the burdens of my economic plight with my neighbor. I do that by being a good steward of my time, talent and resources to the Divine. And I carry it out through my actions of how I treat my fellowman. And I carry out my African theology by using my God-given gifts and abilities to make the world a better place. For me African theology is practicing what I preach. If I expect things to be better I must be the catalyst to make them better. If I want justice, I have to show justice. Similarly, if I want peace, I have to be a peace-maker. The bottom line is that for Black theology to be real in my life I have to make it happen.

The heart and soul of this African American woman is not impervious to her environment. She is the life-line for her family. She is the hope that springs eternal. She is the voice of her ancestors. She is the curator of truth for her faith. And she will not be denied her rightful place at the table. The fight, the struggle, the revolution of her theology will penetrate and reverberate throughout history. As the woman at the well who carried the "Word" to her community; Sherry Denise Bailey is a woman who obstensibly commands her destiny to align with her theology. Correction; not suppression or oppression is the hallmark of her fame. I will correct injustices that I see. I will not oppress the oppressed. And I will fight to empower the helpless. My African theology has not been thwarted. It is not subverted. It is alive and well. It is my identity. It is a call to mutual indebtedness, whereas I invite you to join me in our quest for inclusiveness and harmony. Our souls have been joined together, intertwined, and ingrafted with the blood of the Lamb that is impregnable and immovable. Come let us sit and dine at the Master's table; whereas we can live out what we believe. We can live out the scriptures as it states, "the power of forgiveness over retaliation, of suffering over violence, of love over hostility, of humble service over domination." Jesus won his way to pre-eminence and glory, not by exalting himself, but by humbling himself, to the point of dying a shameful death. We would do good to do the same. By making himself of no account, everyone must take account of him," (Phil 2:10-11).

African theology or black theology is the core of what you spiritually believe. The acts of your kindness, mercy and goodness demonstrate what you believe. In our wanderings and daily activity it is our theology that shows the world who we really are. At the end of the day you can look in the mirror and ask, "did I show mercy? Did I covet my neighbor's possessions? Did I show love? If you can answer, "yes" then we can take pride in our theology. If the answer is "no" then we still have work to do. No one can make you care—it has to be innate. If your theology isn't innate—you're pretty much doomed in my opinion, but don't let my opinion sway you. People can be converted. The bible is a great example of that. Evaluate your own life and when you do be sure to take inventory of your acts of righteousness and justice. If the bad outweighs the good than you are in good company, if not keep the faith and strive to do better. Black theology is here to stay and you can take it or give it away.

Chosen for Potential, Kept by Passion

*O*ur scripture text is coming from Psalms 139:13-14. It states, "for you created my inmost being; you knit me together in my mother's womb. I praise you because I am fearfully and wonderfully made; your works are wonderful. I know that full well." I am going to attempt to answer these three questions. 1) What does it mean to be fearfully and wonderfully made? 2) How are your works wonderful? And 3) How do I know it down in my soul?

What does it mean to be fearfully made? It means I'm one of a kind. I am fly. I am fearless. I am so ferociously put together that I cannot be duplicated, imitated or replicated. If I were to be imitated the person would be a phony, a fraud, a perpetrator. But since God made me in his image there is no comparison. I am an original. I am all-powerful child of the king. And my Daddy doesn't make any junk. To be fearfully made is to be confident in your own skin. It means knowing without a shadow of a doubt that you were meant to be; just the way you are. No comparison, no wavering, no second guessing your worth. You are spectacular! You are a vision of loveliness. And there is no ruler that can measurement your value. You are priceless! You are an exquisite masterpiece that people want to cling to. Know your self-worth and don't allow anybody to deceive or deny you of your birthright.

Do you know who you are? God said you are a chosen people, a royal priesthood, a holy nation. He said, "you are a people belonging to God that you declare the praises of him who called you out of darkness into his marvelous light. (1 Peter 2:9). God adopted you into his holy family. He didn't have to choose you. But he did. Did you know it is your birthright to be chosen by God? Jeremiah said it best this way, "before I {God} formed you in the womb I knew you, before you were born I set you apart." The greatest privilege in being chosen by God is access to him. You have access to your Father any day or night at any time. Before God choose you he had to create you. Psalm 139:13 states, "you created my inmost being; you knit me together in my mother's womb." When God stepped out into nothing and called it something he was thinking about you! God saw your unformed body and took his all-powerful hands and designed the color of your skin; he fashioned the texture of your hair, he composed the shape of your body. He knows all about you. When God knitted you together he had you sewn up in Him. You are God's workmanship! God knows the intricate details of our body and your life. Therefore, he knows every artery, every vein and blood vessel. He put them there. Not only that, but God knows the events of your life from beginning to end, before one of them came to be. Your steps have been ordered by God.

When we look at the creation of man we discover God spoke to himself and his son. In Genesis 1:26, he said, "let us make man in our own image." You came forth because God planned that human beings should be spirit even as he is spirit. When God created the world into being he **made** things and he **created** things. The Hebrew word for "make" is "asha" which means, "to form out of something that is already there." "Brera" is the Hebrew word for "created," which means to "form out of nothing." You see God **made** man from the ground then he **created** man with his breath. Man was nothing until God did something. He blew HIS breath of life into man then became a living soul. And as a result we are Spirit as God is Spirit; because we came out of God. What am I saying? I am saying every living thing that God created was blessed with potential. Most of the potential God gave you at birth still remains within you, unseen and unused.

So let's examine potential. What is potential? According to the author, teacher, evangelist, Myles Munroe, "potential" is "the sum of who you are that you have yet to reveal." Munroe says, God is the source of all potential. He is everything we haven't seen yet. When we describe the characteristics of God we say that he is "Omni" meaning "always" and "potent" meaning "full of power." God is always full of power. **He can always do MORE than he has already done**. You were chosen for the power that's on reserve to be kept by the power that's within you. You may need a moment to grasp the depth of that sentence. God is all powerful. Therefore, all potential is in God. And when you know him you're not afraid to do great things. It's not WHAT you know, but WHO you know that enables you to do great things! When you know WHO you are in God you can do anything. You can resist all things that seek to overcome you or wipe you out.

Author and businesswoman Dr. Wanda Turner says, "power is the ability and authority to recognize or reveal God." With that being said, she further states that women of God have that power. That power is, "having the unlimited, unshakable, unstoppable, unbreakable Spirit of your Father in Heaven." Is that power in your life? Touch your neighbor and ask them is the power in your life?

Verse 14 in Psalm 139 states, "I praise you because I am fearfully and wonderfully made." When you think about being fearfully and wonderfully made it ought to evoke a praise or a shout! Can you conceive it? Can you envision it? Really? God's thoughts are too lofty for us to fathom. Can you imagine he had you on his mind when he was creating the world? What I think it really means is that you have to affirm yourself. You have to vocalize the words, "I'm worth all that!" You have to vocalize that 'He is wonderful! He loves me! He made me like him!" You have to remember that you are a Spirit. Your Spirit will live forever. There are no imperfections in you. Sure we have flaws, and areas to improve on, on the outside, but God sees your potential on the inside. He doesn't see flaws. He sees his workmanship. Ephesians 2:10 states, "for we are God's workmanship, created in Christ Jesus to do good works, which God prepared in advance for us to do." His work is perfect! Those scars, indentations and bruises are there for a reason. They are there to help you remain humble. They are there to make you reflect more of him. If you didn't have them you wouldn't work so hard at trying to cover them up. God is using those scars to perform His work in you. To be fearfully and wonderfully made is to be reverent. It is a position of worship. It is a place of humility and awe. God workmanship should always display his sign, his insignia or his stamp. Being fearfully and wonderfully made is to be a portrait of praise to God. Every time someone looks at you they should see God in you. What does that look like?

Being wonderfully made is knowing that God choose you. Remember his thoughts are not our thoughts; nor or our ways his ways. Thinking that God had you on his mind before you were ever conceived should just blow your mind. The thought of it is too wonderful for us to conceive. But he did. Everything God does is good. To answer the question of how do I know his works are wonderful is to look back at creation. Remember back in Creation when God said let there be light and there was light. And he said "that was good." God said let there be expanse to separate water from water and he called it "sky." Then he said, "that was good." God said let the water under the sky be gathered to one place and it called it "dry ground." And then he said, "that was good." God spoke the sun, the moon, and the stars into existence and then he said, "that was good." God created living creatures according to their kind and he said, "that was good." His works are wonderful because everything he does is good. He said it. We should believe it. So when God speaks that settles all disputes. Nothing more can be added or detracted.

I can just imagine that our God had an executive staff meeting with the Holy Spirit, the Father and the Son. They discussed a matter of great importance—YOU! Imagine if you will; God conversing with Jesus. And God said, "who will be able to project or image? And Jesus said, "man and woman because you created him and you shaped her." God responded and said, "that's good." Look at your neighbor and tell them, "God made you and "it's all good!" He had to take you out of the world to place you in position as wife to your husband. God took the rib from out of Adam's side and then he made woman. Scripture states in Proverbs 18:22, "he who finds a wife, finds a good thing." He brought her to man. And Adam said, "this is now bone of my bone and flesh of my flesh." And God said, the "two shall be one." Genesis 2:25 states, "the man and his wife were both naked and they felt no shame." We must realize that as minister's wives God chose us to stand alongside our husbands and to work together in ministry. Even if you're not a minister's wife you were chosen to serve and work for God. When you've been chosen by God to work for him there is no failure; no condemnation and no shame. God is wonderful. He always has a purpose and a plan. You were chosen for the untapped power God placed in you. You were chosen to perform all things for his glory. You were chosen to be God's portrait of praise. How do I know that down in my soul?

I know it because the last part of verse 14 in Psalm 139 states, "your works are wonderful, I know that full well." You know his works are wonderful because when you think about what you were doing before he saved you—your soul should shutter; you should get a chill down your spine. You perish the thought at the shear mention of that person's name being uttered that you were doing the dirt with. Lord have mercy is now you badge of honor. Praise God for that.

God's works are wonderful you know that down in your soul. Do I have to remind you? Does anybody here remember what you used to do? Do you remember what you used to call yourself? Do you remember how you used to act? But thanks be to God—you're not the same; you have been changed. You don't go to those same places anymore. You don't hang out with the same kind of folks. You don't drink and cuss and fuss like you used to. Now you're a child of the King! He delivered you from addiction. He delivered you from sexual sin. He delivered you from gossiping and backbiting. He delivered you! If that isn't wonderful, I don't know what is. God's Word says His works are wonderful. If you've been set free; you should know his works are wonderful. If you have a testimony; you know his works are wonderful. If you experienced the power of God in your life; then you know his works are wonderful. I know his works are wonderful because he is using me. You know his works are wonderful because he chose you. He could've chosen someone else; but he didn't. He chose you. Praise God that you're chosen. Praise him that he thought enough of you to be his daughter or son. Praise God he chose you to fulfill his purpose. You were chosen for potential because of the power that is within you. You are kept by passion because of the power that's yet to be revealed in you.

In conclusion, you should know that you are a chosen woman and a kept woman or man. You are kept in the secret place of the Almighty! Psalms 91:1 states, "he who dwells in the secret place of the Most High God shall abide in the shadow of the Almighty." We're talking about being chosen for potential and kept by passion. You're a kept woman or man because God is perfection. You're a kept woman or man because of God's blood. You're a kept woman or man because of God's Word. You're a kept woman or man because God is perfection. He is the Savior of the world. He is without sin. There is no spot, blemish or wrinkle in him. He is the Righteous One. He came out of nothing and made it something. He created all things without him nothing was created. God is perfection because he is omniscient. He is all-wise. He is Omnipotent. He is all-powerful. He is Omnipresent. He is everywhere. He is the Way, The Truth and the Light. He is the only one we can have eternal life. He is the Trinity. The Father, the Son, and the Holy Ghost. In him we live, and move and have our being. (Acts 17:28). There is no condemnation or failure in him. Therefore, I can lift my head and be ye lifted up ye everlasting doors and the King of Glory shall come in. Who is the King of Glory? The Lord Almighty. He is the King of Glory (Psalm 24). God is my portion so whenever I get weak I need to go back to the strength of my supply. God's strength is made perfect in my weakness. Thank you all-wise God for knowing more than me. Thank you all-wise God for keeping me. Thank you for delivering me from the miry pit. Thank you that I know who I am deep down in my soul!

I am a chosen woman with potential because of his blood. He kept me. His blood purified me on the Cross, therefore I am not lost nor condemned. His blood sanctified me; therefore I am forgiven and redeemed. His blood changed me; therefore

I am a new creature. His blood covers and protects me from my enemy; therefore I know his mercy endures forever. New mercies I see every morning because mercy watched over me all night long. When I think I'm lost; unloved or unforgiven . . . I can say, "Oh no—His blood paid the cost." I am a kept woman because of God's Word. His word is a lamp unto my feet; a light unto my path. When I'm alone and feel in despair I can go to his Word. And His Word tells me that I should, "trust in the Lord with all mine heart; and lean not to my own understanding, but in all my ways acknowledge him and he will make my paths straight." (Prov 3:5). I am a kept woman because God's Word says he will "keep me in perfect peace whose mind is stead on him." (Isaiah 26:3). God's Word says, "I am your deliverer; a strong tower and your comforter. Who can bring a charge against my elect?" (Prov 18:10).

I am a kept woman because God's Word says there is "no sin that has overtaken {me} except that which is common to man that {he} will not provide a way out." (1 Cor 10:13). I'm so glad that God's Word keeps me. And that Word is living on the inside of me. I'm so glad that my passion is God's Word. Now I can have peace that passes all understanding. Now I can have joy unspeakable and now I can run this race without being weary. I know at the end I will receive a victor's crown that was made just for me; an everlasting, eternal crown, if I don't give up.

Remember you were chosen by God to reveal his power. You are God's workmanship placed on earth to do good works. Remember that you are chosen to reflect God. And you can do all things because he keeps you in his secret place. Allow God to use you—do it today and forever!

The last verse of Psalm chapter 139 reads, "See if there is any offensive way in me and lead me in the way everlasting." God knows all about us. He can deliver us from sin and bondage. He will direct our paths. He will shine like the noon day sun. Allow him to have his way. He will give you more than you need. He is more than able to rescue you from the clutches of evil. Allow him to shower you with his goodness. He is the King of Kings. He is Lord of Lords. He can never fail. His grace is sufficient. And he keeps his promises. God is amazing.

Remember that you are chosen for potential and you are kept by God's passion. He desires for you to give yourself to him so that he can show off his masterpiece. Allow him to dazzle you.

Deeply Depend On God

In George McCaleb book, "Faithful over a Few Things," he says, *"Nearly everything we are about depends on the quality of our relationships: our marriage and family; our friendship; our employment; and our very legitimacy as a person."* He says our greatest and most important relationship is the life changing relationship God calls us to with him. The first component in relationship is people. People matter. People are important. Why are people important? People are important because we are God's crowned creation. God declared in Psalm 8:4-6, "What is man that you are mindful of him? And the son of man, that you care for him? You made him a little lower than the angels and crowned him with glory and honor. You made him to rule over the works of thy hands; you put everything under his feet." WOW! People are important to God. People are more important to God than people are to people. God thinks more about man than man thinks of himself. God said we were made a little lower than the angels and we are crowned with his Glory. Verse 6 says, "he made us to have dominion over the works of thy hands, he put all things under his feet!" HALLELULAH!! God did that for us. That tells me that God truly cares about His people and His relationship with his people.

How is your relationship with him? Do you need a revival? According to your theme it states, "An Extreme Makeover: Transformation by Design: Reviving Our Relationships." My My My!!! It sounds like you not only need one; but you want a better relationship with God and with people. Praise Jesus! We are going to look at our focal passage in Nehemiah, but before we do that let me set the stage.

Many of us are familiar with the book of Nehemiah. We know that he was a wine steward for King Artaxeres. He went to the King to ask him for favor because the walls of Jerusalem had been destroyed. And Nehemiah wanted to rebuild the walls. As I was studying the text God showed me what walls represent. He showed me that walls represent God's salvation and God's protection. In our story, the walls had been broken down for 140 years. And they were burned. Therefore, the people's protection had been destroyed. And they were in a vulnerable position. They were without salvation. They were without protection.

And so it maybe in your own life—you have some broken down walls. Your broken down walls may be an unhappy marriage, unruly children, or financial problems; whatever your brokenness is—God wants you to examine your situation. If you are not where you should be you need to ask God "what" is going on; not why it's happening? You need to ask God; "What" do I need to do to be in right relationship with you (God) and with my brother and sisters?

In our story, Nehemiah's brother came to him and told him the walls had been broken down. Nehemiah was so distraught that he sat down and wept. He mourned. He fasted. He repented and he prayed. In Nehemiah's prayer he asked God for favor. Nehemiah reminded God of the promise he gave Moses when he said he would rescue the Israelites from slavery if they repented and returned to God. Nehemiah was on a quest. He was on a mission to restore broken-ness. In order to that he knew he needed help from God. So he prayed and asked God for favor to complete his task. Nehemiah had success because he began at the right place. He began with God. In the end, God granted success. He granted success because Nehemiah asked in sincerity and in purity of heart. The story ends with Nehemiah reclaiming the people from exile after they been scattered all across Babylon and Judah. It ends with Nehemiah leading the people to recommit their hearts back to God.

So If I were to entitle this message I would entitle it "Deeply Depend on God." To restate your theme again: Extreme Makeover: Transformation by Design: Reviving our Relationships" That's a good theme. Our scripture focus is: Nehemiah 4:6. In my study of this text God spoke to me. He said before we can revive our relationship with each other; we need to go on a reconnaissance mission. A Recon mission allows you to take an exploratory survey of the situation. It allows you to seek out information about the enemy without them knowing about it. Some of us are our own worst enemy and don't even know it (or maybe you do). You see when you go on a reconnaissance mission it allows you the privilege of seeing the situation from a better perspective. It's like flying in an airplane. When you're up in the sky your view of the ground is broader. Your perspective of the situation is clearer because of your position. And since God's position is higher than ours; don't you think we should ask him what he thinks? What does God think of your relationship with him and others?

That is what Nehemiah did before he could start the work on the walls. He went on a recon mission. He went to explore the situation to seek out information.

In chapter 2: 11-13 Nehemiah goes out and examines the broken walls. And he doesn't tell anyone what he's doing until God lays it on his heart to do so. Some of us need to do the same thing in our relationships. When God reveals His vision of his assignment for you—it doesn't mean he wants you to tell everybody. Wait for his timing. Even though the walls were broken down it didn't mean they were going to stay that way. And God is saying that your situation may look destitute, it may even look dismal; but God says you must see your present situation doesn't determine your future position. Your marriage may be shaky; your children maybe acting crazy; and your finances maybe funny; but he wants you to know that's not the end. Your future position is in God. He determines what will happen in your life. God can turn that shaky marriage into marital bliss. He can turn those crazy kids into obedient soldiers. And he can turn your funny finances into financial freedom if you deeply depend on him.

Our dependence on God lies in our ability to trust him and take him at his word. I need to say that again. Our dependence on God lies in our ability to trust him and take him at his Word. And God gave me three words to share with you about how to revive our relationships. Remember we're on a recon mission. Look at your neighbor and tell 'em—"We're just exploring our situation."

The first word God gave me is RECALL. Recalling is simply reminding or remembering. Nehemiah recalled his past sin; his ancestor's past sin and their rebellion. He reminded God of the promise he gave Moses when he had rescued them from Egypt. Nehemiah asked God for two things; (1:11) He asked God to: incline his ear to his prayer. And secondly, he asked God for "favor" with the King. Let's look at Nehemiah 5:1-10. Nehemiah's prayer was sincere, specific and short. It cut straight to the chase. He admitted his wrongdoing and his people's wrongdoing then he prayed for deliverance and restoration. Nehemiah wanted to see his people in one place. And he wanted to see them worshiping God in the temple. He desired for his relationship with his people to be right. How many of you have that sincere desire to see your sisters and brothers alongside you worshiping our Holy God? Are you in right relationship with your brother or sister? Are you willing to be revived? Some of us don't want revival—we rather damn people to hell. What do you mean Sis. Sherry? Every time you seal your lips and refuse to tell people about Jesus and what he has done for you—you're telling them to go straight to hell! And that's cool if you want to do that because there's a place for you in Hell right alongside of them! But I'm talking to those of you who want to be revived! Are you willing to step out on faith so God can rekindle your Spirit? Remember we're just exploring our situation.

In your life God wants you to recall what he has already done for you—how he made a way out of no way. Recall how he brought you out without a doubt. Recall how he showed himself strong when you felt like you couldn't go on. God says, remember, reflect and recall how I have brought you through the valley of the shadow of death. Remember how he brought you through storm after storm and you're still here. Remember how you made it through because he's been keeping you. And remember the relationships that he allowed you to survive through!

When Nehemiah reminded God of his promises; it caused God to act. So it is in our own life. God want us to recall his Word; recall his favor; and God wants us to recall his wonder working power.

In chapter 2, verse 4; the King Artaxerxes asked Nehemiah "what" does he want and Nehemiah answers in verse 5. But not before he prays to God. (don't miss that). Read Nehemiah 2:4-5. The King said to me, "What is it you want?" Then I prayed to the God of heaven, and I answered the king, "If it pleases the King and if your servant has found favor in his sight, let him send me to the city in Judah where my fathers are buried so that I can rebuild it." Nehemiah told the King what God had laid on his heart to do—which was to rebuild the walls. (Remember God's timing). We too can take our cue from King Artaxerxes and Nehemiah by asking God, "What is my assignment Lord?" Ask him: "What do you want me to do?"

You see the devil knows his assignment—steal, kill and destroy. What's yours? It's time to stop playing church! We're in a war! Your life is at stake. You can't come to church—playing church anymore—it's time out for that! God says be about his business. Our somber and traditional practices don't move God. We got to launch a full blown attack against our enemy! He's not going to sit idly by and wait for you to get your war clothes on. You better gear up! Get yourself in position and fight this good fight of faith! After you ask God what is your assignment then wait for the answer. Once you hear God's voice then you can seek out resources because God has already provided "favor."

Verse 6 says, "Then the King with the queen sitting beside him, asked me, how long will your journey take, and when will you get back?" And God maybe asking you today—"how long are you going to be stuck in your current position; stuck in your situation?" And when are you coming back? He wants to use you for ministry like nothing that you have ever done before. God wants us to recall his promises and remember that he will do just what he said. God wants us to recall His Word in Phil 1:6: "being confident of this, that he who began a good work in you will carry it on to completion until the day of Christ Jesus." You can bet what God begin he will finish. When we recall God's Word; his favor; and his power; then we will be in the right position for revival—which leads me to the second word God gave me. Reclaim.

Nehemiah reclaimed his people by asking the King for favor to get the walls rebuilt. We too can do the same thing when we reclaim our rightful place in God's Kingdom. Some of you have been called to teach, some of you have been called to preach, some of you have been called to care for the sick. No matter what the call is on your life—God wants you to reclaim your role; take your position and arm yourself with the Word of God. The people of Judah did it while they were rebuilding the wall. They kept a weapon tied to their waist and a tool in their hand. (Neh 4:17). The God you and I serve wants you to be battle-ready! No matter what obstacle you may face in your life; God has given you the tools and the weapons to stand and reclaim your position.

The bible says, "our weapons we fight with are not the weapons of the world. On the contrary, they have divine power to demolish strongholds." (2 Cor 10:4). And God is saying there are some things in your life he has to demolish. He has to demolish those walls of fear; demolish walls of selfishness, demolish walls of rebellion; demolish walls of strife; demolish walls of anger; demolish walls of competition and covetousness.

In the rebuilding process renovation is required. Renovation means re-building the structure so that it's sound. And so that it can stand up to the test of time. The elements of the weather—like a storm, hell, fire or tornado have to be tested. That renovation project God is working on is you. You are the structure that needs rebuilding! Are you standing on sound footing? In order to reclaim your position you must accept your calling. Your calling involves people—and people require you to have a relationship. That relationship hinges on your relationship with God. When we stand in our rightful position armed with the Word of God—God will allow us to reclaim everything the devil stole from us. He will give us power from on high to demolish every stronghold—and every brick wall that has blocked you from your blessing. We must have the Word of God in our hearts and reclaim the blessings of God. He wants you to reclaim your rightful position in the kingdom. And when you do that—God says revival will take place in the hearts of the people when they stand in their rightful place.

Nehemiah RECLAIMED his people from exile;
Nehemiah RECLAIMED his people from extortion; and
Nehemiah RECLAIMED his people's place of worship in the Temple.

But I must warn you . . . that when you reclaim your position expect opposition; because it will come! And when it comes you need to be battle ready. You need to be able to stand your ground. Look at the opposition Nehemiah and the people faced. (Read Neh 4:1-3). In Nehemiah's day his enemies were Sanballat and Tobiah. These are people in your life who ridicule you; laugh and talk about you when they see you trying to live better or do something good for the glory of God. But you have to keep going despite what people say. Nehemiah faced his enemies. He did it with the right companions by his side. He had a bodyguard, a servant and he had workers. In your own life; God will have the right people by your side cheering you on and supporting you to do the work. If you have some enemies in your life; don't worry—just pray. God will help you to continue to do the work. Check out Nehemiah's strategy for facing opposition.

Chapter 4, verse 4, states, "Hear us, O our God, for we are despised. Turn their insults back on their own heads. Give them over as plunder in a land of captivity. Do not cover up their guilt or blot out their sins from your sight, for they have thrown insults in the face of the builders." You see when the enemy sets up camp around you—you need to speak to God. Don't give credit to the enemy. Go to God and declare, and decree some destruction in the devil's life. We can't be whimpering wimps when it comes to reviving our relationships. We need to stand and stand until our change comes. No devil in hell can defeat you when you're battle ready! We've got to equip ourselves with the Word of God; gear up with the belt of truth buckled around our waist; the breastplate of righteousness; the shield of faith; the helmet of salvation and the sword of the Spirit; as well as our feet ready with the gospel of peace. (Eph 6:14-16).

You see when you're battle ready with your war clothes on you can extinguish all the fiery darts the devil throws at you. We have the power to proclaim, pronounce, and recite the Word of God if we keep ourselves battle ready. You see the Israelites were battle ready. Look at what they did (Read Neh 4:16-18). "From that day on, half of my men did the work, while the other half were equipped with spears, shields, bows and armor. The officers posted themselves behind the people of Judah who were building the wall. Those who carried materials did the work with one hand and "held a weapon in the other".

Verse 18 states, "each of the builders wore his sword at his side as he worked. But the man who sounded the trumpet stayed with me." To be battle ready you must keep your weapon close to your side and the Word of God in your heart. Yeah. God will fight for you but you must have your weapon!

Look at Neh 4:23, it states, "Neither I nor my brothers, nor my men, nor the guards with me took off our clothes; each had his weapon, even when he went for water." That tells me I have to always be battle ready. I don't ever take off my armor. The only way I can be ready for battle is when I have hidden the Word of God in my heart. God already gave you your equipment for warfare. What are you going to do? I came to tell you, we have the victory in Jesus name; if we only seek his face and believe in his Word. When the enemy is on your trail that's the time to go deeper in God's Word. Pull out every scripture that you can find that speaks to your situation. Call it out and keep saying it until it gets into your Spirit and you begin to act on it. The bible says, "the power of life and death is in the tongue, and those who love it will eat of its' fruit." (Prov 18:22). So eat in Jesus name.

In the name of Jesus pronounce praises, pronounce blessings and pronounce miracles into your life. When you do that you denounce the devil's dominion over your circumstances. You can tell the devil that his diabolical deeds will not do you in. I can recall God's word in Psalm 8:4-6 saying, "he made him to have dominion over the works of your hands; he has put all things under his feet." So put that damn devil under your feet!

You see the walls of Jerusalem had been broken down for 140 years; so the city's protection lay in ruin. It might be the same for you. Your life may be messed up from the floor up, but God can take 25-40 yrs of mess; and 25-40 yrs of rubble and ruin and turn that into 52 days of power! Some of us need a "Nehemiah Mentality." Whiners, worriers and wimps especially need it.

Nehemiah was equipped with the right stuff. He was a quiet storm. He didn't say much but when he did speak—it was powerful. Nehemiah was a prayer warrior. Anytime he felt opposition he prayed. Anytime he felt evil he prayed. Anytime he needed direction he prayed. He was a man of action. He was a man of courage. He was a man of God. He was a man of strength. He was a man of power. He deeply depended on God. Each time there was a problem he relied on God solve it. Each time he didn't have the answer he trusted God. Each time he enemies came against him he depended on God by consulting him first before he fought. Nehemiah was no wimp! He stood on God's promises.

One of things I've discovered about God is that he tests his people. **The reason why we go through struggles is because God wants to see if we can be trusted**. Nehemiah went through each of these struggles because God was testing him. Nehemiah's test was fear. God wanted to see if he would high tale it and run when the enemy came; but Nehemiah passed his test. And because of that God promoted him from wine steward to governor. (Neh 5:14). Nehemiah went from serving wine to building bricks of power and protection.

His obedience got him promoted. He stood with the sword at his side; a tool in his hand and a plan in his heart.

What do you have? You know God has given you a vision, a purpose and an assignment for your life. What are waiting for? How long are you going to stay stuck in your current position? How long are you going to stay stuck in your situation? Are you still struggling through your test? God wants to perform a mighty makeover in your life. He wants to renovate you from the inside out. Will you let him have his way? Can you be trusted?

In reviving our relationships we recognize that we must recall God's Word; recall God's favor and recall God's promises. Secondly, we must reclaim our rightful position in God. And in reclaiming our rightful position we will see revival. We will see our broken relationships restored and our broken walls rebuilt. Finally, the third word God said was recommit. He said remind the people of their commitment to me. Recommit. We must recommit our hearts to God. When we do that the work will get done. Remember the promise you made to God? Remember your church Covenant? God wants you to recommit to him. Nehemiah led the people to recommit when they completed the rebuilding project in 52 days. The people asked Ezra the priest, to read the book of the Law (bible) by the Gate; where they had all gathered. They listened to the Word of God and they recognized that it was God who allowed them to complete the wall. And with that their hearts wanted to hear the Word of God. And when they heard the Word they were moved to tears. So they made a commitment.

Hear what they said in Chapter 10 verse 29 it states, "all those now join their brothers the nobles, and bind themselves with a curse and an oath to follow the Law of God given through Moses the servant of God and to obey carefully all the commands, regulations and decrees of the Lord our Lord." The Israelites recommitted their hearts to God. They said they would keep the laws and requirements of God. Didn't you say that too when you accepted Jesus as your Savior? Are you willing to recommit? God wants you to deeply depend on him—not man.

When you recommit your heart to God no work is too demeaning or too great for you to accomplish. Your recommitment will be the catalyst for your change. That change will create in you a burning desire to please God. Pleasing God will be your driving force to be in right relationship with your brother and sister and deepen your dependency on God. As we have seen in Nehemiah's day the people were moved to worship when their work was done. And we see the people celebrating the dedication of the rebuilt walls. They did it because they had recommitted their hearts to God. When you recommit your heart it changes your attitude about worship and you come to celebrate God in a new and different way. You have an attitude of gratitude and your soul rejoices with the truth of God. The Good News bible says "the peoples' praises could be heard for miles" (Neh 12:43b). This tells me when you get in your rightful position and recommit your heart to God; people will see by your walk and your talk and they will know that you are a child of the King.

Look at what God can do in 52 days! In 52 days the burned and broken down walls were rebuilt. Imagine what God can do with you in 52 days?—if you only recommit to his way!

I found some interesting things about the number 52. There are 52 cards in a deck and there are 52 weeks in a year. But what I really found spiritually profound about the number 52 is that we have 52 bones in our feet. And with those 52 bones in my feet I can recall God's Word saying, "I have put all things under his feet"—therefore I have dominion over my circumstances! The walls of Jerusalem were rebuilt in 52 days. And I know whatever circumstance comes my way God has given me dominion over it all. So for you to experience true victory in Jesus; we have to put some feet to our faith; and put some praise in our mouth as the Israelites did when they marched on top of the wall they had rebuilt. They marched, sang and played instruments to the glory of God. They did it because they knew God had granted his success. When you recommit your heart to God he will bless your faithfulness.

In closing . . . . If you deeply depend on God he can do anything and everything. No matter how bad things may seem God can rebuild. He has his Son; Jesus; his Holy Spirit and him to do it. If he can take 140 years of rubble and make it a powerful wall of protection; surely he can take your mess and make a masterpiece. If you're willing to deeply depend on God he can restore your broken relationships. If you deeply depend on God he will make the mistakes in your life into monumental testimonies of his goodness. If you deeply depend on God he will show himself strong in your situation. If you deeply depend on God He can turn your broken finances into bountiful blessings. If you deeply depend on God he can turn your enemies into your strongest supporters. If you deeply depend on God he can resurrect the deadness. If you deeply depend on God he will rekindle your Spirit so that you're on fire for him. Deeply depend on God and he will bring revival. And the revival will begin with you!

Remember to RECALL His Word,
RECLAIM your rightful position and
RECOMMIT your heart to him.

Diamond in the Dust

Why do we love diamonds? We love them because they are beautiful, rare and mysterious. They are known to be a woman's best friend. They are known to last forever. But how much do we know about them? I did a little research and uncovered some interesting facts about diamonds. Permit me to share a few with you. First, I'm going to tell you briefly about the history of the diamond. Secondly, I'm going to tell you about the 4 C's factors that determine a diamond's worth. Finally, I'm going to tell you how we too are like diamonds.

The legend of the diamond says that children were playing in a small village in S. Africa and stumbled upon a rock. They brought it back to the village and a neighbor took it to a trader in town who took it to a geologist. It turned out to be worth a small fortune. This began the diamond excavations in S. Africa. But it is a misconception that diamonds were discovered in S. Africa. The truth is diamonds were found in India first and since that time that have been widely unearthed all over the country including Australia, Zaire, Botswana and Russia.

But how do diamonds form in the earth? Picture this. Thousands and thousands of years ago when the earth had frequent volcanic eruptions these eruptions created magma. This magma also called kimberlite—a hardened igneous rock formed. Inside the kimberlite are intermittent deposits of diamonds. Diamonds are a chain of carbons. Carbon is one of the most common substance on the planet. In one form, its' a simple graphite—used in a pencil, but in its crystallized form it takes on another appearance as a diamond. It is similar to you and I—when we were in our former state of un-repentess. We were filthy rags. Isaiah said, "all of us have become like one who is unclean, and all our righteous acts are like filthy rags; we all shrivel up life a leaf, and like the wind our sins sweep us away." (Isaiah 64:6). But in our redeemed state God says were a chosen people, a holy nation, a people belonging to God (1 Peter 2:9). He even calls us a royal diadem in his hand (Isaiah 62:3).

Diamonds are the hardest natural substance known on earth. They are one of rarest substance thus being the reason why they demand expensive prices. The Greek word for diamond is "adamas" which means "invincible" or "inconquerable." I can recall in God's word when he told us that we are more than conquerors. So anytime someone tries to throw dirt on you— you need to let them know God created me. I'm rare and hard to the core—nothing you do can break me.

Another reason why diamonds are so valuable is because the light they absorb is reflected back outward—if they have been properly cut. That tells me the more I stay in God's Word (which is the Light) the more I can reflect what's in me.

Another interesting fact about a diamond is that there are no two diamonds exactly alike. Once diamonds are mined they are delivered to sorting experts who categorize and assign a value to them. Over 2000 years ago your Heavenly Father created you before the foundations of the earth. He assigned a value to you and he told you that you were fearfully and wonderfully made by his precious hand. Then he said I have drawn you from the rock (Isa 51:1) and now you are a beauty, a splendor to behold like a stone in my hand. (Isa 62:3). A royal diadem is priceless.

In ancient times diamonds were left uncut and mounted into their settings which gave them a dark, deep mysterious look. Later in the 1400s diamond started being cut and polished which gave them sparkle and brilliance. Cutting a rough diamond takes great skills. A well-cut diamond reflects light within itself from one facet to another, from the top to the bottom. The more its cut right; the more brilliant it will sparkle and shine. What does that mean to you? It means God is saying that it doesn't matter how many times you've been cut by man— it doesn't matter how deep your wounds maybe—it doesn't matter how deep they dug the pit for you; even though they meant it for your bad—God is going to work it out for your good (Genesis 50:20). Remember Joseph was thrown into a pit and God elevated him to a palace.

I want to tell you four (4) ways to determine the value of a diamond. They are known as the 4 Cs.

1. Cut—After a diamond has been cut once; it gets cut again and polished and reclassified. The art of polishing a diamond is to maximize its brilliance and fire. In other

words, if a diamond is cut too deep or too shallow it's less brilliant; and less valuable. The message for us is the pain and suffering you've been going through was just enough to polish you for service for the Master—it's for your good.

2. Color—The smallest variation in color makes a big difference in a diamond. Women of God we don't need to be color conscious. In other words, we don't need to be color struck. That means we should love our complexion. It doesn't matter how darker or light your complexion is to another sister. God made us all unique and he wants us to be "transparent" so people can see through us and see Jesus. Colorless diamonds are the most popular and sought after stones. Nature makes diamonds of all colors of the rainbow. But you should know black diamonds are the most rarest and valuable.

3. Clarity—Most diamonds have natural imperfections or inclusions; known as "flaws" to us. We as women of God know that we have flaws. We're not perfect. But the good news is God didn't call us to be perfect—he called us to be set apart; chosen—a royal priesthood, a holy nation; a people belonging to God to declare his praises of him who called us out of darkness into his wonderful light. (1 Peter 2:9)

4. Carat—The carat is the weight or size of a diamond. After a diamond is weighed it is given points. For example, a one carat diamond is the equivalent of 0.2 grams which

equals 100 points. I'm here to tell you that you shouldn't be obsessed with your size or weight. It doesn't matter how big or small, you are. It matters how you see yourself. I can recall the bible saying in Heb 12;1, that we should, "lay aside every weight that so easily entangles us; and let us run with perseverance the race marked out for us. Verse 2 says, "fix your eyes on Jesus; the author and perfector of your faith." I'm here to tell you that your life may be full of flaws; your character may be filled of imperfections; but God says he can still use you. It doesn't matter how big or small you are—God says you have purpose. It's his purpose that you must fulfill in this season of your life. We are dearly loved daughters. We know our past, we are living our present and God has our future all sewn up in Him. We need to dust ourselves off and emerge as the beautiful splendor he created us to be.

Fashion Me a People

$\mathscr{A}$ key issue of a "Fashion Me a People" by Maria Harris speaks of church people living out their pastoral vocation by making a difference in the world. The church is a people called to a "mission." That mission is "sending." In the role of pastoral care we are called to serve in diverse ways; in particular five ways are identified: 1) koinonia, meaning community; 2) leiturgia, meaning prayer and worship; 3) didache, meaning teaching, 4) kerygman, meaning proclamation and 5) diakonia, meaning outreach. Moreover, Harris states that pastoral vocation has three components: 1) hallowing, blessing, remembering and works of teaching, prayer and preserving tradition; 2) calling to bring institutions of our world into account and we are to claim our authority to do that; and 3) as prophetic people we are to speak the word of justice and embody God's pathos. We do that by continuing to grieve over human suffering and sin.

The key issue I found relatively surprising and innovative were the three tensions pastoral vocation poises. Harris says tension is good and without it collapse is inevitable. She describes personal versus communal being one, local versus global being second, and clergy versus laity a third. Harris states the church is guilty of demonstrating, "individualism" rather than "personalism." Human maturity is shattered due to force and power of personalism, according to Harris. She postulates that all human beings have the right to abundant gifts by the Creator, however this belief collapses when applied to the marginalized, the disenfranchesized, the poor and women. Rugged individualism is really a celebration of the "powerful, wealthy and White men," according to Harris. She further states the greatest contribution of personalism is to be a "person with (i.e., when we are in community and communion with one another"). And that our existence as humans in community is personhood, so whenever there is a denial of one human; the community falls short.

The second tension in pastoral vocation exists between local versus global tension which Harris says should be autonomous. The local congregation should be "answerable only to ourselves before God or we as a universal organism with each local unit as a cell are necessarily related to all the other cells worldwide." Within that same vein, Cilako M. Mulango states in Bediako's book, "African Theology" that African primal religion has two notions: 1) worldly and 2) wordliness which encompasses God and man in abiding relationship with the divine. And the destiny and purpose of humans is to the universe. Man is a global agent whether he wishes to believe it or not. I think as Christians we must view the global needs of our world. Consequently, if we ignore them, there are detrimental ramifications that we will face locally.

To simply it further, I would say it is the notion of translatability which carries the meaning of continuing to be yourself while immersed in another religion no matter where our origin of the world. It is synonymous with universality. When we view the Christian religion through the lens of "translatability" it is a smoother transition to depict Christianity as "culturally indefinitely translatable," according to Andrew Walls. In other words, we continue to adopt and practice our religion no matter where we are.

The third tension of pastoral vocation is clergy versus laity. This tension has been set forth by our inappropriate division of ourselves. Using the language "lay" connotes negativism. It is not a distinction of who we really are; rather it is a distinction of how and where we live out our vocation. For example, Paul was a tentmaker and Peter was a fisherman. They lived out their pastoral vocation while gainfully employed. In Ephesians 4:11, it states, "God called some apostles, some teachers, etc.," The bottom line is we need each other. It is not a spitting contest of the have and the have-nots; the ordained or non-ordained or the illuminated and the ignorant. More importantly, it is the recognition that both roles; clergy and laity overlap. Therefore it begs the need for one another. It is my opinion that this author's viewpoint coincides with my own. I am all for equality. Pitting a layperson against clergy is undignified and degrading. Our churches can be served best when we learn to work in harmony with one another and loose the title, "layperson."

Harris presents church education in a new framework. She basically asserts that the new paradigm shift is not exclusive to a special body of people or special place or time. But it is all people in all communities connecting with the Divine. I wholeheartedly agree with her. Asserting curriculum means to "run;" taken from the Latin word "currere." If we as ministers are going to "run" with the Word of God we must make sure our curriculum is sound, whole and universal. In other words, make it applicable to the listener. There are four areas in church education she presents: 1) agency, 2) activity; 3) participants and 4) knowledge/obey laws. In the old model agency was that done by an individual or an "official" of the church. In the new framework it can be performed by the community. Activity was done by the institution or through indoctrination; whereas the new framework presents activity through education and community. The participants in the old framework were children—the new model encompasses the whole community. The direction of the old model was knowledge and obey laws (church lore); while the new framework engages the community in the midst of living within our world.

Practically speaking, I believe this plan is doable. It can be implemented within the church setting. For far too long we in the church have modeled Christian education from a vacuum and not as a living organism. We would do well to toss out the old and embrace the new, but maintain the traditional value of the old. Fred Newman and Donald Oliver charged that teaching Christian education should not be restricted to the concept of school. They examined the "missing community." They said how this one essential component can bear much fruit. These men argued for three contexts: 1) school, 2) wider community and 3) studio or work. In other words we, as a people can benefit when our education is widen through various settings;

not just in the classroom. Oliver and Newman challenged our use of metaphors. They suggest we reclaim our stand on curriculum. The words, "reform, restructure, and recognize" are superimposed to dismantle the old ideology and usher in the new. These men believe the nature of curriculum is fluid; not set and that the church can broaden its horizon than just by schooling one.

Using Acts 2:32; 42-47, Jesus stood up and said that we all are witnesses (kerygman). Further stating, "they devoted themselves to the apostles' teaching (diadache; kerygma) and fellowship (kononia) to the breaking of bread and the prayers (leiturgia) . . . and all who believed were together and had all things in common (konionia) and they sold their possessions and goods and distributed them to all, as any had need (diakonia). By applying this model the author believes that "curriculum is already present in the church's life: it is in teaching, worship, community, proclamation and outreach," according to Harris.

I must agree with John Mbiti in his work, "Theology in African Christianity," that the church universally must re-indentify itself. After all Latin American theology took its roots from Ecumenical Association of Third World Theology in 1976. And Englebert Mveng spoke of spiritual liberation versus liberation theology. He said conversion history is that which is germane to a person's culture, context or nation. Therefore, we must see Christian education as a cross-cultural convergence of celebration where learning takes place not in a straight line, but through interlocking, interconnecting circles that are constantly evolving.

As a minister, seminarian and a person in my community it is incumbent upon me to live out my religious convictions. How that plays out I am not sure, however; what is certain is that until we explore new possibilities we will be trapped in the "could've, would've, should've mentality." In our local churches and places of worship we can integrate this new model of curriculum by inviting and engaging the community to participate with us. Harris says the curriculum of the church is the life of the church. I adamantly agree with her. By empowering the people to live out the five key elements of worship: didache, leiturgia, koinonia, kerygma and diakonia; we as a community can visualize the three offices of Jesus being: priestly, prophetic and political. We must see education as a continual exchange of our lives. And when education stops we stop. Much more can be said about this subject; however I choose to implore you to seek out your own answers and practice Christian education in your local community.

In conclusion, it is my supposition to execute Christian education in my local church. It could be a mangled mess if I were to go at it alone. Thankfully that is not my plan. I have led ministry for the past eight years as a pastor's wife and I know the intricate details, pitfalls and triumphs of delivering Christian education. The tasks is noble at best and not for the weak-hearted or timid. But not many other duties merit the shear exuberance and singular satisfaction one derives from one person being enlightened by the word of God. I anticipate the future of the church universally. It will be "the whole body of Christ . . . joined together by every supporting ligament, growing and building itself up in love, as each part does its work." (Ephesians 4:16).

Gift of Redemption

*R*emember what it felt like to receive a gift you weren't expecting? The exhilaration you felt was matchless beyond compare, right. It's kind of like the excitement you experienced as a child on Christmas morning. Well the gift of redemption is similar to that. Think of it this way—when the Lord gives you a gift—it is something that you never want to part with. I would like to share with you my view of this subject.

The Lord is Jehovah. He is Our Sanctifier. He is Our Redeemer. The blood of Christ redeems us from the guilt and penalty of sin. (1 Pet 1:18-19). What is redemption? According to Unger's bible dictionary redemption is to deliver by paying a price or to take away. It also means to buy back from slavery and to remove from the marketplace permanently! Hallelujah! Jesus Christ permanently removed us from the world of sin and placed us above in the heavenly realm with him. We have the power and the authority (right) to overcome any trial or obstacle that attempts to entangle us. It's all in the blood of the Lamb!

The Greek word for redemption is "lootros." Literally translated it means to loose or set free. In other words, the blood of Christ set you free from your sin. It is that blood that takes away all sin. It erases and expunges the stain of sin. Our sin forces us put our heads down in shame. It cuts our fellowship in two with our Father. And it results in death. But the good news is the power of the Holy Spirit delivers us from the dominion of sin based on what happened at Calvery. (Rom 8:2; Gal 5:8). What happened at the Cross sets us free. This means sin no longer controls us. We are covered because of the blood of Christ.

Jesus Christ paid the ultimate cost. He paid the ultimate price to redeem us from the law. The law convicts. It sentences us to death. But what the law was powerless to do Jesus became the atoning sacrifice for our sin. He made sin powerless and we became victorious over our sinful nature. We were bought while we were still in sin then removed out of sin because of Jesus' sacrifice—his shed blood on Calvery's Cross. Thank you Jesus that we have a right to the tree of life. It is because of that self-less act that we are no longer slaves to our sinful nature; instead we are heirs of the promises of God—just like Abraham (Gal 4:6-7) we inherit all the promises of God. (Gal 3:29). Those are shouting words! Hallelujah!

There are four rewards of redemption I want to share with you. In reality these rewards are gifts that are yours when you join the family of God. First, the reward of redemption is **wholly from God**. There is nothing more powerful on earth than Jesus' precious blood—his efficacious blood paid the penalty for our sin. You cannot get this gift from anyone else. It comes only from God. It doesn't come from a psychic; a mine or a buddah. It cannot be channeled through science. It's not in the universe. It is in the Master of the Universe. His precious blood ensured that we wouldn't be lost. It is the most effective substitute for our sin. There is no greater example of love than the picture of the Cross. Jesus was hung on a cross, he died on a cross, and he was lifted up from a cross. The Master's blood was shed for your sins and mine. And nothing can separate us from his love. (Rom 8:35).

Being complete; being whole comes from God alone. Everything we ever did wrong and will ever do wrong has already been atoned for because of Jesus efficacious blood shed on Calvery's Cross. Therefore we are not destroyed.

The gift of redemption is free. When you come to Jesus he freely pardons you of all sin. And God said in his Word, "whosoever shall humble himself as a child, the same is greatest in the kingdom of Heaven." (Matt 18:4). When you come to Christ you receive redemption from your sins. It is your free gift. And only God can give it.

The second reward of redemption is having a **personal relationship** with the Lord Jesus. There is only one way to God and that is through His Son. The Son gave his life for you and me. Redemption is the key that unlocks the door and sets us free. It is freedom from sin and death. The way to experience redemption is to accept the Father and the Son. Redemption's gift is the assurance of having your bad deeds erased; your evil thoughts annihilated and your dirty and devilish tongue sanitized by the blood of the Lamb. Remember redemption is to deliver by paying a price. God paid the ultimate price for your wrongdoing and mine. He sacrificed his life on Calvery's Cross. Your redemption comes through the person of Jesus the Christ. He is the author and finisher of your faith. There is no other way to be saved. The bible says, "I and the Father are One, no one comes to the Father except through the Son."(John 10:30). In the book of John, he goes on to tell us, "For God so loved the world that He gave His only begotten Son, that whosoever believes in Him will have everlasting life." (John 3:16). Redemption comes through a person. His name is Jesus Christ. It's about having a personal relationship with him.

The third reward of redemption is your **blood bought connection**. When Jesus was pierced in his side on Calvery his precious blood can streaming down. His precious blood dripped down his face when the soldiers placed a crown of thorns on his head. His precious blood oozed out when the seething soldiers whipped him with horrendous spikes delving into his innocent flesh. His precious blood came shooting out falling insanely on the ground. Each time we see the Cross it should remind us of the blood stained sacrifice Jesus gave so that we wouldn't be lost. Jesus gave his life. Jesus gave his precious blood. Jesus' precious blood is the propitiation from our sins. It is the ONLY suitable sacrifice for our sins. It is this precious blood that saves us, erases our sin, sanctifies us and nullifies the law. It seals us in the heavenly realm and justifies us before the Father. There is nothing more effective than the precious blood of the Lamb of God. One drop will wipe away all sin, whether action, word or thought. Our blood bought connection is too expensive of a price to pay to let it go to waste.

Finally, the fourth reward of redemption is **power.** Jesus has all power in heaven and earth. He has all dominion. And he has all authority. God gave it to him. (Matt 28:18). He is the King of kings and the Lord of lords. And Jesus gave us this same power. He reigns supreme over heaven and earth. The power of redemption is found in Christ. When you accept Jesus you too possess this power. Being a child of the King entitles you to divine power and privileges. These divine privileges far exceed the world's standards. They surpass anything you can imagine acquiring down here. And your privileges are supernatural. They encompass the power to speak to your giants, your enemies and your nay-sayers—commanding the enemy to fall, to be cast down and return to the pit of Hell where he belongs. When you've been redeemed by the blood of the Lamb you have the power. You have the power to trample on serpents. You have the power to command mountains to crumble. You have the power to call those things that be not as they were. You have the power to tear down strongholds and to walk in victory in all areas of your life. Jesus has delivered us. We have the power! It's all in our tongue. (Prov 18:22). We must recognize as blood bought believers; we too can do all things through Christ who strengthens us because he redeemed us. Praise Jesus for his infinite gifts and unfailing love. Will you accept your reward of redemption?

$\mathscr{P}$ersevere $\mathscr{U}$nder $\mathscr{P}$ressure

$\mathscr{I}$n life we're going to have struggles. No matter how good you live, trouble will come. No matter how bad you live, trouble will come. The question is . . . how are you going to deal with the trouble? We feel pressure daily. Some of us are pressured by our families to provide. Some of us are pressured on our jobs to meet deadlines. Some of are pressured to get to work on time. Some of us are pressured to figure out how we're going to make our ends meet. We can admit that pressure is not foreign to any of us—we can all relate to the anxiety of pressure in our lives. I would even venture to say that our children feel pressure. Whether they're big or small—I'm sure they've experienced the weight of pressure in their lives.

Today, I want to talk about "Persevering Under Pressure." Our sermon spotlight is on the book of Esther, in particular chapter 4, verse 12-14,

The central idea of the text is God's timing is always right.

The book of Esther is full of timing. In other words, it's packed with numerology about when things happen. This is demonstrated when Esther rose from being a slave girl to becoming Queen of Persia in 7th year of King Xerxes rule and the 10th month (Esther 2:17). Lots were drawn to determine when the Jews would be destroyed. It happened in the 12th year of the 1st Month (Adar). Lots are known as "pur" in the Jewish culture. (Esther 3:7). The lot to kill the Jews happened in the 12th month of the 12th year. (Esther 3:7b).

We're talking about God's timing. The order describing how to kill the Jews took place on the 13th day of the 12th month of the 12th year according to chapter 3 v.13. Esther became queen in the 7th year of King Xerxes rule; but her time to defend her people didn't come until the 12th year. She had been queen for five years.

My first point is this . . . we must "**walk in sync with God's timing.**" You may be in a position at work, at church or in your family for so many years; but your time to shine has not yet come. We must remember it's all in God's timing. You must walk in sync with the Master—in his timing you will be elevated. In order to be elevated—you have to persevere under pressure. You got to keep fighting, keep striving, keep being faithful, don't let anyone or nothing knock you off course. You may be struggling now; but stand under the pressure—God sees all and he knows all and he will not leave you alone. Just wait on his timing.

Thirty days had passed since Esther had been summoned by the King. Everyone knew if the King did not extend his royal scepter you could not come into his presence. Esther had to go to the King at the right time; because if she didn't it would cost her—her life. Remember it's all in God's timing.

Some of us want things to happen in our own timeframe. We're not willing to wait—but God says wait on him. Allow him to go ahead of you—when you do—you will see the deliverance of the Lord.

Take King Jehoshaphat for example. In the bible God's timing is always right. Before King Jehosophapt went into battle (2 Chron 20:17), he had the wisdom and faith to seek God's face for direction. Just like Esther did. Jehosophapt called the people to fast and pray. When he took the time to inquire of the Lord; God delivered him and they were victorious! If you want to be victorious you have to walk in sync with God's timing! Walking in sync with God doesn't mean you're going to be exempt from pressure. Esther wasn't. Think about it.

Esther was a young girl, not more than 12-13 years old when she had been thrust into the limelight. She went from obscurity to popularity in a very short time. You think she didn't feel pressure? She was under pressure to keep her nationality a secret until the right time. Think about the stress she was under. First she had being taken away to live with a distance relative after her parents died; then she was herded through a harem of girls like cattle; for a man to look at her like she was a "suit" for him to wear. Then Esther had to undergo a yearlong worth of beauty treatments where the eunuchs in charge of her instructed her on how to act, what to say and how to say it. Everything imaginable was extended to Esther because of her beauty. But yet she still felt the weight of pressure. She was given a husband she didn't know; given servants to command she didn't know; and she was entrusted to live in the King's palatial palace where I'm sure she didn't know her way around. But she had been chosen for such a time as this.

The bible speaks about timing a lot. In the Book of Ecclesiastes God speaks about, "it's a time to laugh; a time to cry, a time for war; a time for peace; it's a time for everything under the sun."(Ecc 3:4). Even Jesus said in the 7th chapter of John; "the time had not yet come for the Son of God to be glorified." It all goes to show you timing is everything. We must walk in sync with God's timing to have victory in our lives. Esther waited for God's timing and when she did the Jewish people were spared from death. It happened according to God's timing.

You may be feeling like your time to shine has not yet come. But I want to encourage you today—your time will come. Hang on in there—if you walk in sync with the Master you will be victorious! God has not forgotten. He sees all and knows all. But you must walk in sync with his timing.

My second point is **we must persevere under pressure**.

No matter the odds against you—you can persevere. What is persevering? It's simply pressing your way through difficult or severe situations. That's what Mordecai did. Even though he knew he had saved the King's life; he wasn't rewarded for his allegiance right away. But he didn't get mad and throw in the towel; he stayed in the race. We need to do the same. Stay in the race and persevere under pressure. After Haman was elevated to 2nd in command and the King decreed that everyone was to kneel and pay honor to Haman there was pressure. The pressure came because Mordecai refused. This enraged Haman. He was so outraged that he devised a wicked plot. He didn't just want to kill Mordecai; but all the Jews. So the King issued a decree to have it done.

The central idea of the sermon is that we can persevere under pressure.

Mordecai showed his ability to persevere under pressure by sitting at the King's gate lamenting over his people. He did it loudly and boldly. He did it without regard to what people thought. He persevered under pressure. That's what we must do. Some of you have given Satan too much credit and authority in your life. You need to turn the table on that dog and occupy and possess what belongs to you! We get so caught up in the "what" of our lives that we get off track. We should focus on the "why" of our purpose. See you're no threat to the devil "complaining" and "proclaiming" about "what" has happened to you. You're more of a threat to him when you begin to operate in your purpose. Let me tell you how you can persevere under pressure.

When people tell you—you can't; persevere with Phil 4:13, "I can do all things through Christ who strengthens me."

When people tell you—you're not good enough; persevere with Psalm 139:13, "I am fearfully and wonderfully made."

When you don't have enough money and your resources are all dried up; persevere with 2 Chronicles 29:11-13, "Everything in the heavens and the earth is yours Oh Lord. And this is your kingdom. We adore as being in control of everything. Riches and honor come from you alone and you are the ruler of all mankind. Your hand controls power and might and it is at your discretion that men are made great and given strength."

When people diss you on your job and discount your abilities; persevere with Psalm 46:1, "God is my refuge and strength; an ever-present help in time of trouble." You need to let them know that you are a perseverer and an overcomer!

When people call you out of your name and talk about you like a dog; persevere with Isaiah 43:4, "I am precious and honored in God's sight and he loves me."

Then tell them what Isa 62:1 says, "I'm a crown of splendor a royal diadem in the Lord's hand."

When your creditors take your car, your house and your stuff; persevere with Isaiah 61:7, "instead of shame, I will receive a double portion and instead of disgrace I will rejoice in my inheritance, because I will inherit a double portion of the land and my joy will be everlasting!"

When those ruthless dogs come after you trying to steal your faith, your joy, your health; whatever it is—you need to persevere with James 1:2 . . . "the testing of my faith develops perseverance. Once perseverance has finished it work I will be mature and complete not lacking anything."

Then tell them what James 1;12 says, "blessed is the man who perseveres under trial because he will receive a crown of life."

You can tell those ruthless dogs what 1 John 5:4 says, "I am born of God and because of that I have overcome the world. That is my victory, even my faith!" Hallelujah!

Not only are we perseverers, and overcomers; but we are more than conquerors! Romans 8:37 says, "we face death all day long; but in all those things we are more than conquerors!"

We're so bad that we can call our spiritual homies and persevere with Lev 26:8, "five of us will chase a 100, a 100 of us will chase a 1,000 and our enemies will fall by the sword right before us."

On top of all that . . . 2 Chronicles 20:27 says, "the Lord will give you a reason to rejoice over your enemies!" HALLELUJAH!!!

Mordecai was able to rejoice over his enemies because the trap Haman set to destroy the Jews; he and his 10 sons fell into. The gallows he built to hang Mordecai was the same noose they tied around his neck. There's a lesson in here for us. We need to be careful we're not setting people up for failure that will lead to our own demise.

Some of us think that when things aren't going our way—we can get in there and sabotage someone else's work; or help God out—intervening where we don't belong will lead us to being cut off and cut out.

Jesus is the ultimate perseverer! He persevered under the cross so that none of us would be lost! He persevered to complete the assignment his father had given him. He perfected perseverance and he made His Father's joy complete! Are you willing to do the same? Jesus said, in John 16:33, "in this world we're going to have trouble, but take heart! I have overcome the world." If Jesus has overcome the world that means I can overcome too. He told us greater things we will do because he goes to his Father. So if he did it, you can too!

When Jesus speaks that means something. So if I'm smart I should adhere to what he's saying. He also said in Rev 2:11, "we are overcomers by the blood of the Lamb, and the word of our testimony." If you never go through anything how can you experience the joy of victory?

What have we said thus far? Our first point is . . . we must walk in sync with God's timing. The second point is . . . we must persevere under pressure and finally our third point is . . . **we must stand for justice**. We must stand for what's right no matter what. MLK said, "if we don't stand for something, we'll fall for anything." That was Haman's problem. He couldn't stand that Mordecai wouldn't bow down and pay him homage; so he devised a wicked plot to kill all the Jews; but it backfired on him. And he fell into his own trap.

As men and women of God we must stand for justice. God is justice. He is always right. He never changes his mind. His word is the same yesterday, today and forever. He cannot lie. When he acts who can reverse it? God is all-wise; all-powerful and always present. We were created by God to bring Him glory. (Isa 43:7) So shouldn't we act like him? Yes we should.

We should stand for and represent our Father at all times. When we walk ahead of God we fail; when we walk behind God we miss opportunity; but when we walk with God we are victorious!

I have to admit sometimes our faith wavers. We suffer from what I call temporary spiritual amnesia. We forget how good God has been. That's the time we should saturate ourselves with the Word of God. And allow Him to wash away all our worries. When Esther prayed and fasted God revealed his plan. She waited for the right time by walking in sync with God. She persevered under pressure and God spared her life and the lives of the Jews. Esther stood for justice because it was right. And the revelation came when she said in verse 17, "if I perish, I perish." Mordecai's message was just information to her until God showed her a glimpse of the destruction of her people. Then her moment of enlightenment came. She experienced an epiphany; and the revelation overshadowed her situation and she was able to stand her ground and stand up for justice.

The message for us today is even when your world is crumbling—you got to stand for justice. You can persevere under pressure. We can stand because God gave us the ability to stand. He delivers justice and we can too. His word tells us, "for I, the Lord, love justice." (Isaiah 61:8). God's word also says in Ephesians 6:13-14 says, "therefore put on the full armor of God, so that when the day of evil comes, you may be able to stand your ground, and after you have done everything to stand. Stand firm then." Esther stood because she spent three days fasting and praying. She was fortified in the word of the God; she was ready and prepared to stand and deliver the word God had revealed to her.

We, as children of God can stand in the power of God when we spend time in the word of God. Esther's stand was so strong that it reverberated throughout history. Jews today celebrate "Purim" because of her stand. What about you? Will people talk about your stand in history? The songwriter wrote, "on Christ Jesus the solid rock I stand, all other ground is sinking sand." If you're going to be victorious you have to stand for Christ. When you stand for Christ he will reward you for your faithfulness. Persevere under pressure and watch God deliver you. Psalms 39:14 says, "many are the afflictions of the righteous, but the Lord will deliver him out of them all." Esther stood on the word and the word delivered her and her people from destruction. God can do the same for you; when you walk in sync with God's timing; persevere under pressure and when you stand for justice. We are called by God to do something GREAT for God. Stand in the strength of his word and be amazed at what you can do. Isaiah reminds us that we "are called priests of the Lord, you will be named ministers of our God." (Isaiah 61:6). And because of that God will grant us grace and favor. He reaffirmed his word in Isaiah 61:7 when he stated, "instead of shame my people will receive a double portion, instead of disgrace they will rejoice in their inheritance." God has given us all that we need for life and eternity. Stand in the power of the Holy Spirit and receive the gift of grace. Esther did it with her people. We too can do it with our family and friends when we activate our faith.

Surviving Suffering is Purposeful

$\mathcal{T}$he lyrics to a popular song states, "must Jesus bear the Cross alone and all the world go free? No, there is a cross for you and there's a cross for me." As cross bearers we must suffer. Christ suffered all the way to the grave bearing his cross. Therefore, we are not exempt from suffering. It is a requirement for the journey. No one is left out. Romans 5:3 states, "we also rejoice in the sufferings, because we know that suffering produces perseverance; perseverance builds character and character builds hope. And hope does not disappoint us; because God has poured out his love into our hearts by the Holy Spirit whom he has given us." And we need to have a bodacious, unwavering and perpetual hope that will energize us into an excessively abundant reality.

We suffer vicariously through the sufferings of Christ 1 Peter 2:21 states, "to this you were called because Christ suffered for you, leaving you an example that you should follow in his steps." It is a part of discipleship. We have been given a blueprint, a model, an example of suffering through Christ, therefore as his children we must follow our father's footsteps. In other words, we must go through similar misery and strife if we are to be called his children. The last five words of verse 21 states, "to this you were called." You were called to this journey of suffering for the sake of Christ! My. My. My. Many of us don't want to endure that part of the journey, but it is unavoidable. It is unrelenting. It is unmistakably going to happen. So what is the good news? I'll tell you in a minute. But first I must let you know why we should endure suffering with rejoicing.

We should endure with rejoicing because God told us to. Joy is simply regret turned upside down! You can have joy in the midst of your circumstances when you know without a shadow of a doubt that things are going to work out. You know things are going to work out because of your faith and trust in the Lord. Trouble doesn't last always. And when your faith is grounded in the Lord than you know that he is able to do "more than all we can ask or imagine, according to his power that is at work in us." (Ephesians 4:20). We can rejoice because God is near. He hears our cries for mercy and grace. And he is able to grant us peace and joy that surpasses all understanding." (Philippians 4:7).

1 Peter 2:23 states, "when they hurled insults at him, he did not retaliate, when he suffered, he made no threats. Instead he entrusted himself to him who judges justly." How many of us can say we don't want to lash out at people who have done us wrong? It's hard to do. We must admit if somebody steps on our toe or calls us out of our name, we are prone to retaliate. It's a natural defense mechanism. However, we who are Christians are called to follow the example of Christ. What's that example? Part B of that verse states, "entrust" yourself to him who judges justly/righteously. We should consider it all joy whenever we face trials and suffering as Paul says, (James 1:2)

and anticipate the joy and glory of God's will to be revealed in our lives. (1 Peter 4:13). The songwriter wrote, "trouble don't last always." And the Psalmist wrote, "for his anger lasts only a moment, but his favor lasts a lifetime, weeping may endure for a night but joy comes in the morning." (Psalm 30:5). So take courage and confidence in knowing that the pain will soon dissipate and joy is coming soon!

We really don't know what joy is unless we experience some pain and suffering. Our pain and suffering should prompt us to rejoice and praise God more. That's the real test of discipleship. If you are going through something the world should be able to tell whether you are a Christian based on how you deal with your problem. The question is, "do you moan and groan about your problem or execute a plan of action while praising God through it all?" As called out people of God we must suffer. And as called out people of God, we must entrust God to carry us through it to cement His purpose for our lives. We should also remember what John said in 16:33, "in this world we are going to have trouble, but take heart, {you can} overcome the world." You can overcome the world because Jesus did already. And we are imitators of him! So you can shout right there.

1 Peter 3:9 states, "do not repay evil or insult with insult, but with a blessing, because to this you are called so that you may inherit a blessing." As children of the King in right relationship with God and our fellowman, we should exemplify godly character. Our interaction with others should reflect godly traits at all times. Therefore, when someone insults you or mistreats you as a Christian we should give a blessing! That

is easier said than done. Most of us would have some choice words for the person that insulted us. However, scripture clearly says to NOT return insult for insult; rather give a blessing. When we experience the vicarious sufferings of Christ we eventually will endure hardship, grief and trouble from others. When that happens we must carry the mark of a disciple. We must conduct ourselves with compassion and love; speak a word of encouragement; turn the other cheek; humble ourselves and excuse the other person's actions. If you are truly walking with God you will be able to do that. I didn't say that it would be easy. But we should be a bigger person and not others get to us! But show them God's love despite of their imperfections and ours too.

1 Peter 4:14 says, "if you are insulted because of the name of Christ, you are blessed; for the Spirit of glory rests on you." WOW! That's good news! If you face trials and suffering for the sake of Christ than you are blessed because God's glory rest on you! What an honor! What a privilege! So that tells me that I shouldn't run away from trouble or pray for deliverance out of it; rather I should welcome and expect it! What I need to do is make sure I'm walking in the way of God because scripture clearly states if you're insulted because of the name of Christ—I should be glad because I know God's glory is being revealed in me! Don't get it twisted. Your actions must be in alignment for us to claim that benefit.

Verse 16 of that same verse says, "if I suffer as a Christian do not be ashamed, but praise God that you bear that name." It is a privilege and honor to be called a child of the King. So let's remember trouble is inevitable. The real test is how you bear up under it. The result of your trial should produce two things. It should: 1) perfect your faith and 2) mature you spiritually.

Verse 19 says, "those who suffer according to God's will should commit themselves to their faithful Creator and continue to do good." We have a common command and a mandate to do good for God's sake.

Finally, I want to give you the good news of suffering. The bible says in 1 Peter 5:9 "resist him." Stop there. Resist who? Resist the devil. It continues with "Standing firm in the faith because you know that your brothers throughout the world are undergoing the same kind of sufferings." The good news is that you are not alone. It is not peculiar. It is not strange. It is not a phenomena or an out of body experience. It is just life. No matter how long or how short of a time we've been walking with God we are going to have trouble. People all over the world are going through similar trouble. Your pain and your trial is not unique. Matter of fact it's common. You are not the only person who lost a job; had their home foreclosed; filed bankruptcy; got a girl pregnant; had a baby out of wedlock; lost a loved one; smoked dope; went to jail or prison; or stole money from others. No. You're not the only one who is suffering. No! By no means! We all have a common enemy. He is called the devil. It is his mission to take you out. It is his mission to reap havoc and make you lose your mind. It is his mission to drive you insane; or cause you to snap; twist off or cuss people out. It is the enemy who would have you to believe there is no hope—you should just throw in the towel and give up. It is the enemy who wants you to turn on your family; to give up on your marriage or to stop giving and serving in the church. It is the enemy who wants you to have a pity party; to close yourself off from the world and declare a depression. It is the enemy who wants to keep you in despair. He wants you to be prone to flying fits and maniacal rages of anger. It is the enemy who wants to sift you as wheat. But God has prayed for you to endure the test. (Luke 22:32). You have to declare to the devil that he is powerless. You have the power to defy the odds and cancel his vicious attacks. After all you are a child of the King! The devil is no match for a strong warrior like you. Serve him notice now! Tell him to get behind you. And stomp the mess out of him. Stand firm in your faith. Take charge. The power is within you! The bible says, "His power is made perfect in our weakness." So don't fret, don't lament regrets, get to stepping and dancing on the devil's head while you're singing praises to God. You are more than a conqueror!

The bible says, "your enemy the devil prowls around like a roaring lion, looking for someone to devour." (1 Peter 5:8). Are you going to let him devour you? Are you going to let him steal your joy; snatch away your family; evaporate your finances? Are you going to fight back? Are you going to stand firm? Stand boldly. Stand in the power of the Holy Spirit. Stand with Jesus. You can do all things through Christ who strengthens you. The good news is that God will bring you out. You will be better than before. The good news is your present position doesn't dictate your future destination. The good news is that God is able. The good news is that God can never fail. The good news is greater is he that is in you than he that is in the world. (1

John 4:4). The good news is there is no trap the devil can lay for you today that God cannot release you from.

Remember Daniel in the lion's den? God is more than able to extinguish, annihilate and eradicate any disaster that attempts to ensnare you. You have to remember that suffering is for your good. It will produce exponential growth in your life. You got to see it through the Master's eyes. God can do all things. He cannot lie. He is your comforter, your fortress, your shield and your buckler. He can position you to defeat all enemies; foreign and domestic. Hallelujah! God is able. Have you tried him lately? He is the God of another chance. Yes, I said another chance. Let's face it. We blew our second chance, third chance and so on until the Master came on the scene. He is Jehovah Mekaddishkem. He is the Lord who sanctifies. He cleanses our sin and helps us mature. God will remake you. He will reshape you. He will transform you. He will shock the hell out of you! He will mesmerize you with his Majesty. He will make your enemies your footstool and have them scurrying in shame. God will defy logic and evoke sweet peace! The sooner you realize that suffering is purposeful—you can stop your whining and start praising Him for his goodness!

I just believe there are some prayer warriors in the house who can declare God will bring you out. I believe there are some committed soldiers who will not let the enemy steal their joy. I believe there are some committed soldiers who will not let the enemy confuse them; baffle them or reek havoc in their homes. I believe there are some committed soldiers who will not let the enemy destroy their marriage; their church; or their family. If I have any true men and women of God let me hear you say, "I'm taking it back!" Everything the devil stole from me, I'm taking it back. Joy is ours! Love is ours! Forgiveness is ours! Restoration is ours!

Some of us can't experience true joy because we've been playing church too long. We know the right words to say, but we don't walk in his ways. As church folk we know church protocol, but do we have power? I'm sure if I said certain words you could finish the sentence for me. Let's test it out.

God is good _____. I'm blessed and highly _____. I'm too blessed, to be _____.

And we know the church protocol to prayer. Let's test it out.

Lord, keep me from all _____, _____ and _____. Lord, I thank you that you didn't make the bed I laid down in last night my _____. Lord, I look to the hills from whence _____ my help.

We can pray church prayers so well while we're trying to sound so sincere, but do we really believe what we are saying? For instance we say, "I thank you Father that you've been my heart-fixer and my mind _____, you've been a heavy-load _____.

You see what happens with church folk is we fall into a pattern, a certain rote memory that is void of any real power. It is impotent. What's up? You know when your prayers and your heart is right with God. You can get a prayer through, but if not you're just like a rocking chair. You're making a lot of movement but you aren't getting anywhere. You need a breakthrough. You need an answer from the King of Kings and the Lord of Lords. You need help! When we begin to focus on our relationship with God and not our religion then we can experience a breakthrough. God wants you to enter into his presence. You can have access immediately and instantly if you only try. Call on his name.

Is there anybody here who knows what I'm talking about? Has God done anything for you lately? Has God shown up in your life lately? Have you seen his wonder working power? Has God show you himself today? Is there anybody here who can unequivocally attest to his goodness in your life? Is there anybody here who seen how he intervened and granted you a pardon in the midst of mayhem? Have you seen him release you from destruction? Have you seen him cease the enemy from prancing on your peace? If so, then you ought to be able to stand up and say Amen!

I know God is awesome. He is all that and some more. And when you have really caught a glimpse of his presence and goodness you can't tolerate church protocol anymore. You won't be able to stomach empty platitudes and mundane prayers from church folk anymore. But you will be able to petition God; activate your faith and allow him to grant mercy and be attentive to your request. You will be able to access God's heart and receive His immediate answer, his blessings, and his direction for your request. Remember God looks at the heart; not what's in your head. The bible says, "for the eyes of the Lord are on the righteous and his ears are attentive to their prayer, but the face of the Lord is against those who do evil." (1 Peter 3:12). Are there any righteous folk in the house today? Holler if you hear me! Amen. Remember surviving suffering is purposeful. Now, run and go tell that!

The Power of Forgiveness

*W*hat is forgiveness? Forgiveness means to send off or away. It is the process of separating the sin from the sinner. What is power? Power is the ability to do or to act. Forgiveness should be a part of our daily lives. It's mandatory in your prayer life. Without forgiveness and repentance we can't get our prayers through to God. Why? It is because unforgiveness blocks our connection with the Father. Don't take my word for it, look in your bible.

In Mark 11:25, it says, "And when you stand praying, if you hold anything against anyone forgive him, so that your Father in Heaven may forgive you your sins." So that tells me that if I want God to hear my prayers I have to forgive what you did to me. And to take it even further I must ask you to forgive me for what I did to you.

Does the scripture really mean "anyone" when it says if I hold anything against anyone I should forgive them? Yes it does. Does anything really mean "anything?" What if a person looked at me the wrong way or stepped on my toe . . . is that anything? Yes, of course it is. But what if that person really did something hurtful to me and I'm struggling with forgetting and forgiving them, then what? I would say to you the same scripture applies. You know when you're harboring unforgiveness in your heart. And it's just not healthy or right. Harboring unforgiveness is like having a large stone or rock lodged over your heart. It blocks your progress. You're not functioning at your best because you've allowed this stone to block your potential, your power, your present and your future. For your own good; you must let it go.

Consider the blockage a stone or rock. Now think about what a rock is. There are three kinds of rocks; 1) igneous; 2) sedimentary and 3) metamorphic. For thousands and even millions of years little pieces of the earth have eroded. Pieces of earth have been broken down and worn away by wind and water. These little bits of our earth are washed downstream where they settle to the bottom of rivers, lakes and oceans. Layer after layer of eroded earth is deposited on top of each other. These layers are pressed down more and more through time until the bottom layers slowly turn into rock.

Metaphorically speaking, ask yourself what type of rock have you allowed to cover your heart?

The igneous rock is a fire rock and it is formed underground or above ground. When underground the melted rock called magma becomes trapped in small pockets and the magma turns into an igneous rock. Above ground these igneous rocks are formed due to a volcano eruption. An igneous rock is formed when the lava cools above ground. What eruption occurred in your life that caused an igneous rock to form over your heart? Is there some trapped unforgiveness you've been harboring?

Secondly, we have the sedimentary rock. These are rocks are usually stratified. They are fine-grained and sometimes composed of fragments of older rocks. These smaller rocks are derived from pebbles, sand, angular fragments, shells or clay. Many sedimentary rocks also contain fossils. A fossil is petrified dirt that has been around a long time. Do you have a fossil rock covering your heart?

Finally, we have the metamorphic rock. A metamorphic rock is a rock that has turned or "morphed" into another kind of rock. What's unique about this rock is that is used to be a sedimentary or an igneous rock; but because the rock was under tons and tons of pressure (which fosters heat), the rock couldn't take the heat so it changed. How much pressure did you endure that caused you to change?

Remember when Jesus' body was laid in the tomb? There was a large stone that blocked the entrance to the cave. No one could get in, nor could Jesus get out—so was the thought. But if you read your bible in Mark 16: 3-4, it says, Mary Magdalene, Mary the mother of Jesus and Salome had come to the tomb to anoint Jesus' body. And as they were on their way they asked each other, "who will roll the stone away from the entrance of the tomb," (v.3). Verse 4 says, "when they looked up, they saw that the stone, which was very large, had been rolled away." The stone had been rolled away. Who rolled the stone away? Jesus? Was it an angel? We don't know do we? But what we do know is that Jesus wasn't there—was he? What am I saying? The point I'm making is that you—have the power to roll the stone of unforgiveness away.

I would rather roll the stone away and receive God's best rather than to suffer without him and live lifeless.

Another thing about forgiveness is that it is for saints. It's really not for aints. When you were born again you immediately invited the Holy Spirit to live within you. Therefore, because the Holy Spirit resides on the inside you can no longer act the same. Before you would say or do anything without guilt or shame and it didn't bother you. But now, you're not the same. You just can't go and curse that brother or sister out. In the past, it didn't bother you that you didn't do what you said, or that you set up your sister to fall because you didn't like her. Today, you are a new creature in Christ Jesus and you are commanded to love. You are commanded to forgive. That means you are required to do, think and be about your father's business.

Our theme scripture is in Colossians 3:13; it says, "bear with one another and forgive each other; just as the Lord has forgave you, so you also must forgive." (NRSV) So you see the reciprocation in this verse? It says we must forgive each other. It's a two way street. When my sister has wronged me, I must forgive her. And when I have wronged my sister I must ask her to forgive me. (my my my doesn't that sound like a child of God?) We can't live according to our former sinful nature. Christ paid too high of a price for us to fall back down that slippery slope of sin. After all, what we're really asking for is mercy, right? Isn't that what God showed to us? If so, we should be quick to forgive. We shouldn't be quick to hold a grudge. Listen to what God's word says about mercy. In Hosea 6:6 it says,

"I desire mercy, not sacrifice." We must remember that our Father in heaven has so much more in store for us when we walk in obedience to His will. Anyway, you do want your prayers answered, right? Therefore, we must practice obedience.

Verse 14 ties all this together and sums up the point about forgiveness. It says, "above all, clothe yourselves with love, which binds everything together in perfect harmony." Clothe yourself with love. It really takes love to forgive. If you don't have love . . . you are lost. God is love, God gave love and God shows us love. We can too. After all, the bible tells us in James 4:17 that it is a sin not to forgive. It says, "knowing the right thing to do and then not doing it is a sin." We must forgive one another because it's right. And if we want to be in right standing with God and get our prayers answered it's a requirement.

If you look further in James 5:16 it says, "Admit your faults to one another and pray for each other so that you can be healed. The earnest prayer of the righteous is powerful and effective." (NRSV). Admitting your faults to each other simply means I have to say something to you. I can't just think it in my mind. I have to sincerely, honestly and humbly ask you to forgive me. When I do that I am being obedient to God. And he hears my sincere prayer. He will answer. Keep in mind, there is no hurt on earth that heaven cannot heal. When we remember what God has done for us we must forgive others, so that our Father will forgive us. (Col 3:13).

Finally, there are three points I want to make about forgiveness. The power of forgiveness will:

- set you free;
- give you new life; and
- will redefine your purpose.

Forgiveness is power. If you want power you must forgive. Power transforms you. It will set you free. Once you speak words of forgiveness to another person you are immediately transformed. Evil, hatred or rage cannot fester in your heart. The power of forgiveness is as strong as the power of love. Try taking it like medicine and see the effects it will have on your life. It will supernaturally change your demeanor, your countenance and how you see yourself. When you operate in forgiveness it will change you dramatically. There is only thing stopping you from experiencing true power. That one thing is unforgiveness. Simply put if you want to live an abundant life; exercise forgiveness daily. The old adage that states, "you reap what you sow" applies with forgiveness too. The more you pardon the other person's mistakes the more others will give you a pass when you hurt them. Being set free is more than absence from bondage it is a mental choice of tossing our disappointments to the Master. He is the Chief Executive Officer for disintegrating pain and disappointment. Let Him have it so that you can be free.

Try taking it like medicine and see the effects it will have on your life. It will supernaturally change your demeanor, your countenance and how you see yourself. When you operate in forgiveness it will change you dramatically. There is only one thing stopping you from experiencing true power. That one thing is unforgiveness. Simply put if you want to live an abundant life exercise forgiveness daily. The old adage that states, "you reap what you sow" applies with forgiveness too. The more you pardon the other person's mistakes; the more others will give you a pass when you hurt them. Being set free is more than absence from bondage—it is a mental choice of tossing our disappointments to the Master. He is the Chief Executive Officer for disintegrating pain and disappointment. Let Him have it so that you can be free.

Forgiveness will give you new life. Once you let go of ill-feelings and stop harboring animosity and resentment towards another person for what they did or did not do to you—you are stepping into a new realm of living. Having new life is like waking up on Christmas morning and finding everything you wanted waiting for you. It gives you a new perspective and resolve about approaching life. There is no comparison to having new life when you have been trapped in a dismal defeatist existence. The resiliency of bouncing back after a child has been punished is similar to what it feels like to have new life. Each of us want to protect our children; but we also punish them when they disobey. It hurts our heart to punish them, but as children do; they forgive us and continue to love us even after they've taken their punishment. If a child can forgive his parent shouldn't an adult be able to forgive another adult? It may be that you should see your pain as a child sees it; then allow the Master of Universe to administer his healing balm to take away the pain. It is powerful and it only takes one dose.

Forgiveness will redefine your purpose. It is no secret that forgiveness can catapult you into a higher dimension than you have ever experienced before. And the only way to know that is to experience it. I cannot begin to enumerate the countless times I have had to forgive in my own personal life. As a result of forgiving it kept me from destroying my life. When my ex-husband falsely accused me of having a handgun; I was jailed for two days. It was a lie, but I chose to forgive. It was at that moment that God was redefining my purpose. Rather than acting out of rage and resentment I choose to forgive. When God saw my actions he manifested His glory. As a result my life was redefined to align with the Master's purpose. All bars were broken and the yoke of enemy was released. It was in the sincere-ness of my heart that I was able to forgive and free myself from pain and shame. God gave me a new destiny to fulfill. I am still on that journey of discovery. I am not certain what all it will entail, but I am enjoying the ride of a life-time. Without forgiveness I would be nothing. Without forgiveness I couldn't write, recite his word or live in abundance. I forgive because I want to live. You should forgive because you want all the power and blessings that come with it. Allow God to show you how it is done. Forgiveness will unlock the key to your future.

The Steps of a Good Man are Protected By God

Today, I was given this theme to speak on. I believe as Christians we already know that God orders our steps. No matter how long or short you've been a Christian you know that God has your back. Most of us know him as the panacea of life. He is our Redeemer. Some say he is a Keeper. Jesus is a Sustainer! And others say, Jesus is a heavy-load sharer! In the word of God, it tells us that, "Jesus is the Way, the Truth and the Light and no one comes to the Father except through the Son. (John 14:6). If you're going to walk with the Lord you should know that he has predestined and ordained every step you're going to make even before you were in your mother's womb. Do you know Him? More importantly, does Jesus know you? If so, then you know who is protecting your steps. The theme you have given me is, "the steps of a good man are protected by God."

Psalms 37:23-24 states, "the steps of a good man are ordered by the Lord; and he delighteth in his way." Verse 24 states, "though he fall, he shall not be utterly cast down: for the Lord upholdeth him with his hand."(KJV). The text suggests that you have to be a good man or woman for the Lord to watch over your steps. As I was meditating and reading this scripture I asked the Holy Spirit to reveal what he wants me to say about this subject. The Holy Spirit said speak to the people about my *peace*, my *protection* and my *provision*. You see in this particular chapter; David is sharing lessons he learned from walking with God. He shares what happens when you apply godly principles to your daily life. We too can take advantage of that same wisdom by applying those same principles.

Permit me to read the New Living translation. Hear what it says, "the steps of the godly are directed by the Lord. He delights in every detail of their lives." Verse 34 states, "though they stumble, they will not fall, for the Lord holds them by the hand." The Message translation says it this way, "If he stumbles he's not down for long, God has a grip on his hand." In order for us to extrapolate the three godly principles God wants us to apply to our daily lives we have to look at the 37th chapter as a whole. Go to verse 4, look where God says, "delight yourself in the Lord and he will give you the desires of your heart." Your desires encompass your wants and your needs too, doesn't it? The requirement to receiving the desires of your heart is being a follower of Jesus. In verse four the Lord commands us to delight in him. In verse 23 he says, "he will delight in us." When will the Lord delight in us? When he sees that we are walking according to his directions.

It is like when the Israelites were coming out from bondage. God led them by a pillar of cloud by day and a pillar of fire by night. That was his covering for his people. As long as the presence of God was covering them—they were protected. His presence was in the cloud. Therefore the Israelites had peace. That's the first point I want to share with you. God says **He will be your peace**. Otherwise how could the Israelites sleep all night without knowing where they were going to find their next meal? They could do that because God gave them peace. Jesus promises to give you peace.

Look at Psalm 37 verse 11, "you will enjoy great peace." (NIV). The KJV says, you "will enjoy an abundance of peace." Not just regular peace, but "great" and "abundant" peace. Any child of God knows that even when the storms of life are raging if you can just get some peace; you can weather the storm a lot easier.

Proverbs 3:5 states, "trust in the Lord with all thine heart and lean not to thine own understanding, in all your ways acknowledge him and he will make your paths straight." The key is to trust. If you trust in Jesus you will have peace in your life.

Psalm 37:3 states, "trust in the Lord and he will delight in you." Peace is a result of trusting God. Every time you see the word "*trust*" in the bible you should think of the Cross; and remember Jesus paid the cost at the Cross. That ought to provoke you to trust Him. And when you do trust him; He will give you peace that surpasses all understanding. (Phil 4:4-7).

He is your Jehovah Shalom. He will give you peace. When the Israelites walked across on dry land at the end of chapter 14 of Exodus; the bible says the "people feared the Lord and put their trust in him and Moses his servant." The Israelites had peace because they put their trust in the Lord. God wants you to have that same peace. But you have walk according to his purpose.

Not only will He give you peace . . . Secondly, Jesus promises to give you **protection**.

Look at Psalms 37 verse 14. It states, "the wicked draw the sword bend the bow to ring down the poor and needy, to slay those whose ways are upright." But verse 15 states, "but their swords will pierce their own hearts, and their bows will be broken." God is saying when the enemy sets up camp all around you—and everything seems to be going to hell in hand basket that's when Jesus is saying "**I will be your protection**." He will not allow any harm to come near you.

Proverbs 12:21 says, "no harm befalls the righteous."

Jeremiah 29:11 states, "I know the plans I have for you—to prosper you and NOT to harm you; but to give you a future." Jesus is Jehovah Nissi—our protection. He is our Banner and our Shield. We belong to Him. Therefore, we should serve the devil notice anytime he comes against us—we need to let him know that he has already been defeated! The reason the devil is defeated is because my bible tells me "no weapon formed against me shall prosper." (Isa 55:22)

1 John 4:10 states, "the one who is in you is greater than the one who is in the world."

In the case of the Israelites the Lord protected them by a pillar of cloud and a pillar of fire. When the Israelites were trapped with the Red Sea in front of them and Pharoah's army behind them God became a wall of water to protect them. He will do the same thing in your life. He won't allow the enemy to do you any harm. You may be damaged a little bit, but you won't be destroyed. It's only when we veer off the beaten path is when we get into trouble.

As I was traveling in my car one day I noticed a few cows in a pasture. They were encamped together eating grass. As I drove passed I noticed what was keeping them in the pasture was the fence. The fence represented their protection. God is saying like the fence was protecting the cows he will protect us.

So far, we have shared that not only does the Lord provide peace, not only does he provide protection, but finally, Jesus promises to be your provision.

Look at Psalm 37 verse 19. It states, "in times of disaster they will not wither, in days of famine they will enjoy plenty." KJV states, "they shall not be ashamed in the evil time; and in the days of famine they shall be satisfied." *Plenty* and *satisfied* are the equivalent of **provision**. No matter what you stand in need of God says he will supply. Men and woman who walk with the Lord need not worry about where their next meal is coming from or how they're going to pay their bills. I hear God say, "I will supply all our your needs according to his riches in Christ Jesus." (Philippians 4:19). That is provision.

Ephesians 3:20 states, "he will do exceedingly, abundantly more than we can hope, think or imagine." God can do that because we are walking according to his plan. Jesus is our Sustainer, He is our Provider, and he is our Peacemaker. He is our heavy-load sharer, whatever we need he will provide. He is Jehovah Jireh—our provider. The only requirement is to walk with him.

Even after the Israelites were delivered from bondage they faced another trial. They traveled in the desert for three days without any water. And they were thirsty. God led them to a river that had bitter tasting water. After the people complained and moaned to Moses the Lord told him to throw a piece of wood in the water. He did. And the water immediately turned sweet. The message for us to take away is that even though you walk with the Lord; that doesn't exempt you from bitter trials. You need to know that the painful trials you are facing are not to punish you; but are there to teach you and help you to grow. Just as the wood changed the water from bitter to sweet; the cross should remind you that God can take the bitterness of your life and make it sweet. Be like the tree planted by the water and recall what David said in Psalm 1:3, "which yields its fruit in season and whose leaf doesn't wither. Whatever he does prospers." No matter what God can take disaster and turn it into decadence. Our objective should be to keep the faith and run the race. God is able to change the bitter to sweet.

Remember your trials are the Father's will. In your desert experience know that blessings and growth will follow you. Psalm 92:2 states, "the righteous will flourish like a palm tree;

they will grow like a cedar of Lebanon." We need to walk where he leads us; listen for his voice and remain faithful to the end. Then we can watch God show up and show out in our daily lives. It's about trusting the Master's plan and having the wisdom to do it. He will continue to order our steps. He can be trusted. And he never changes. He will give you peace. He will give you protection. And he will give you provision.

Trials are Truth Serum for Christians

We are living in trouble times. One need only turn on the TV or click on the internet and find doom and disaster plaguing our world. Just think about it. Mexico's outbreak of the swine flu has spread globally touching places as far as Hong Kong. Sri Lanka is calling for a cease fire; Rome is fending off pirate attacks and here in the United States we are trying to rebound from an economic recession. Yes. Is it any wonder why so many have consigned themselves to crime, despair or suicide? The great scholar Nietsche said, "whatever doesn't kill you will make you stronger." And how many times have you heard, "no pain, no gain." Or maybe you've heard "trouble don't last always?" What were those people drinking when they coined these words? Even our author James tells us, "consider it pure joy when you face trials of many kinds." I don't know about you, but I don't feel gay or gitty when tragedy strikes. I find it problematic. I find it paradoxical. I have trouble wrapping my brain around that. Yes. You would have to be an alien NOT to know our world is deteriorating. Virtually no one comes out unscathed by trials. And yet we are told by James to consider it pure joy! How ludicrous! How asinine! Personally, I am sick of the whole damn lot—oppression, depression, suppression, and concession. Who in their right mind will tell someone I wish you more trials and by the way—the best is yet to come? How ridiculous! I am greatly disturbed by this pericope in scripture. So much so, that I decided to delve deeper into to uncover the mystery of trials. I invite you to journey with me as we discover why should we respond with joy in the midst of trial.

First, let us begin by getting some background on James. We know from scripture James was the half brother of Jesus and Jude. He was a major Leader in the Jerusalem church. And he was the Keynote Speaker at the Jerusalem Council. What I love about James is his straightforward tone. He is brief, but effective. And his words pack a punch. Yes. In times of trouble we need a no-nonsense word that cuts to the chase.

Many of us, if not all of us at one time have felt abandoned by God. Whether it was Satan injecting doubt or if it was self-imposed—we are all familiar with trouble. Trials makes us wonder what is lacking in our life? What is the purpose behind them? I am sure the Israelites wondered the same thing. After leaving Pharoah's tyranny only to be left out in the wilderness with Red Sea in front of them and Pharoah's army behind them I am sure they wondered about their fate. And I am sure even when Job wondered about his fate. He was scarred with boils blistering his body, his lips were sun-parched, and his body was racked with pain; yet he knew he would come forth as pure gold. I believe they were convinced that **God's plan is worked out in the midst of our trials**. Just as an athlete trains and conditions his body to win—we must endure tough trials to win the race of life.

I must admit at times it seems like a **duality of reality**. In other words, it doesn't make sense. It is a paradox. How can you tell a hungry child whose belly is growling for food to endure the trial? It's really joy turned upside down. How do you remain joyful when the world keeps dishing out pain? The painful scars of memory keep you dismayed. Did Blacks slaves invite Master to give them more beatings so that can experience more joy? Did the parents of the Columbine shootings offer shouts of praise when their children were senselessly gunned down? Yet, James words are relevant in the first century just as they were today. He implores scattered Christians to maintain their faith. He invites them to see their trials as **opportunities**; rather than **obstacles**. The duality of reality is that trials show us that our faith is real. James argues that trials come as a spiritual **test of our faith**. Trials are a part of life. And for life to have meaning and purpose we will encounter three stages of trials.

The first is assurance. The Bible states if you have trouble, cheer up God is keeping his promise. John tells us, "in the world you will have tribulation; but, be of good cheer, I have overcomethe world." (1 John 4:4). We can have the blessed assurance that God will take care of us. Our trials bring us closer to Him. Anytime you start something for God the Devil will bring trouble.

Look at Paul, he was sent to a dingy, rodent infested and feces filled prison yet he was called to preach. He didn't pray for God to remove him; he submitted to the trial and because of it we have beautiful epistles. John was banished to an island in Patmos and because of that we have the book of Revelations.

John didn't question why God brought him there. He submitted to the trial. They murdered Stephen because he was a believer, but out of his death came the conversion of Saul of Tarsus. Harriett Tubman was a woman Liberationist, and she didn't give up because it was too tough! No. She pointed a pistol in the freedom seeker's face and said, "move or die!"

Our problem as Christians is that we pray and then complain when God answers our prayer. We may ask God to increase our faith; or help us to be more humble; then when we are faced with a hard trial we wonder why. I believe these Heroes and Sheroes of Faith could respond to trials with JOY because they knew God's plan is worked out in the midst of trials. James tells us, "perseverance must finish its work so that you may be mature and not lacking anything." (James 1:4).

We will do well to remember Paul's words of encouragement that states, "all things work together for our good." (Romans 8:28). God is still on the throne. He ever cares for His Own. His promises are true. He will not forget you. So quit asking why and praise him that Romans 8:28 is still in the book. Quit trembling and trust! Quit pouting and praise! Quit running and rest! Quit worrying and wait. Quit berating and believe!

As we uncover the mystery of trials we must enter Stage 2; which is **endurance**. What happens to most of us is in the midst of trials our FAITH gets misplaced and needs recovering. And we're going to need some reinforcement to propel us through this season. I submit that we have the tools to do it. It is through **endurance**. Just like the athlete who knows the secret to winning is to subject himself to tougher competition, we too must do the same thing. What am I saying? I am saying in order for us to "not lack anything," God has to purge some imperfections out of our life. Those imperfections can come in the form of:

- Arrogance;
- Anger;
- Jealousy
- Selfishness
- Unforgiveness and more

Just like sandpaper is rough. So is life. But the roughness of the sandpaper produces brilliant and beautiful carves sculptures. We as believers must endure. We must go through the fiery furnace of trials just like the Hebrew brothers, Shadrach, Meschach and Abendego. Endurance strengthens our spiritual muscles. And we become better equipped when the next trial comes.

You remember the story of how King Nebuchenezzar ordered the fire to be turned up seven times hotter than usual? All of this was to prove their faith in God. They went into the fire fully clothed and securely bound, but when they cam out three things were evident. Not a hair on their head was singed. The burned their shackles and the Lord walked with them in the fire! The same three things can happen for Christians in our fiery trials. First, the trial works out for your good. Second, the fire sets us free from the shackles of carnality that hinder. And third the presence of the Lord is very real and precious in the fire. Isaiah said "when you walk through the fire, you will not be burned, the flames will not set you ablaze, for I am the Lord, your God, the Holy One of Israel will be with you." (Isaiah 42:2b-3). So the next time you feel the heat of affliction; thank God He is consuming the imperfections in your life.

Finally, the third stage of unveiling the mystery of trials is **maturity**. When Christians cannot endure trials and grow in their faith they are lacking something. James calls that something, "wisdom." He suggests that you can get wisdom through prayer. "If anyone lacks wisdom, he should ask God, who give generously." (James 1:5). Facing trials and enduring them leads to spiritual growth—that's **maturity**! Prayer brings God's wisdom to bear. It helps us make good choices in tough times. Solomon tells us "the fear of the Lord is the beginning of wisdom." Those same words are etched above the door in the Stitt Library here on our seminary campus. Wisdom is not attained through being smart; rather it is a gift from God. God is the storehouse of wisdom. And prayer develops our faith and enables us to be more confident in God; knowing that he loves us. Only people whose faith is shallow question God's existence and goodness. These people go to church but they are not believers. We call them hypocrites. James calls them double-minded. That person struggles with a real relationship with God. But a person whose faith is strong is unmovable. They know God's plan is worked out in the midst of trials. James reminds us that God responds generously when we call on Him.

"Got any rivers you think are uncrossable? God any mountains you cannot tunnel through? God specializes in things thought impossible, And God can do what no other can do."

No matter what trial you're facing today remember God is working it out for your good. Remember we must all go through trials. **The key is to endure and mature.** Look at it this way—God can turn your midnight into day! He can show you the Way! Just remember He is always there. He will NOT put more on you than you can bear. We are examples of His precious love. And the best way to show our faith can be summed in these words:

"I rather see a sermon than to hear one any day. I rather one should walk with me than just show me the way. The eye is a better pupil and more willing than the ear, Advise may be misleading, but examples are very clear. And the lectures you deliver may be very fine and true, But I rather get my lesson by observing what you do, For I may misunderstand you and the fine advise you give, But there is not mistaking how you act and how you live."

Turning A Negative Into A Positive

We are all familiar with the saying "when times get tough, the tough get going." And that is exactly what the disciple did in our story today. In Mark 14:26-31 the disciples deserted Jesus during a tough time. The scripture states, "when they had sung an hymn, they went out into the mount of Olives. And Jesus saith unto them, All ye shall be offended because of me this night: for it is written, I will smite the shepherd, and the sheep shall be scattered." One can only wonder why faithful followers would become detached deserters. The problem they had back then is similar to our problem we have today. We have to decide if we are going to be a part of the world's church or Heaven's church. Yes. We are here in the world. And perceive God to be up there. Yet, we still have to decide if we going to be a part of:

- Inculturation or salvation;
- Be inclusive or exclusive;
- Be a part of the oppressors or liberators;
- Choose death or choose life;
- Be deserters or imitators—

In our story—The Lord's Supper; a joyous occasion is cut short by an arresting indictment by Jesus who announces, "you will all fall away." He is prophesying betrayal to his would-be benefactors. Well, here is their opportunity to turn a negative into a positive.

You and I have been given that same opportunity. Are we going to be for Jesus or against him? Are we going to be in denial or face reprisal? Jesus declares, "strike the Shepherd and the sheep will scatter." I pondered what that meant. I believe it means in life, whenever we are faced with a tough decision, the answer we are seeking hinges on what our faith is rooted in. In other words, if you are a WARRIOR believer; your faith is your ROCK. You can stand strong even when the storms of life want to knock you down. But on the other hand, if you are a wimpy believer you will crumble; you will scatter; you will turn and run for cover when the heat is turned up or the pressure of life becomes overwhelming.

And I'm sure the disciples thought they were WARRIOR believers; but their faith went limp during a tough time. Even though they swore their loyalty to Jesus to the point of death; they missed the mark. They dropped the ball. They were in the negative. But the good news is Jesus saves deserters. He saves deniers and betrayers too. Which means there is hope for you and me.

We are faced with tough decisions every day. Will I read and maintain my momentum in Seminary or will we enjoy the fellowship of friends and family? I submit to you today that Jesus has the power to turn your negative into a positive. He can turn what has been a thorn in your side into triumph. Because Jesus died on the Cross we are not eternally damned.

But he didn't just die. He rose from the grave. He rose with all power to save! So no matter how many times we drop the ball, Jesus saves us all! He turned deserters into disciples. He can turn your negative into a positive.

What's In the House?

I'm mad as hell and I'm not taking it anymore! If you are like me you should be mad too. Enraged. Inflamed with the apathy we display in worship. You should be outraged with the religious spirit we bring to God's house week after week. I'm here to talk to you about worship. I'm going to talk about three things. 1) hindrances to worship, 2) how we should worship and 3) the rewards of worship. I believe, our problem is that we bring a lack of reverence to the Most High God in church. We bring pre-scripted praise songs and so-called devotion to God's throne without a moment's reflection in prayer. The nerve of us so-called Christians calling what we do worship. We need a spiritual shaking and revelation about worship.

Let me drop some knowledge on you about what God revealed to me. As I praying over this sermon I asked God what he wants to reveal to his people. God said worship was never intended for natural man. Worship is for (him) God alone. My question to you is: who are we to superimpose our religious practices and our order of service on God and then have the nerve to call it worship? We need to ask God what he expects and then allow him to reveal it!

Some of us want the semblance of worship without the sanctity of worship. In other words, we want the tapestry of worship—the outside adornment, but we don't want the holiness that is required with worship. Holiness is living a righteous life. It is an inward dedication to God. Holiness speaks of your character and your conduct. Worship is about what you believe about God. It is what you believe about the character of God. If you believe God is a healer and a restorer you can worship him authentically.

Let me tell you what a worshiper is. A worshiper is a person who can praise and serve God no matter what their circumstance in life. They're not going to stop coming to church or stop serving God because somebody made them mad. A worshiper will move heaven and earth to get to God's house. A worshiper will not run away from a problem; but will face it head on with God by their side and with the Word of God on their lips. A worshiper will not crumble when things get tough and throw in the towel. A worshiper will fight their way back to God to get empowered to face the world. Are there any worshipers in the house?

And there is a difference between a worshiper and a praiser. You see a praiser praises God for WHAT God has done. But a Worshiper worships God for WHO he is. As a Praiser I can shout, sing and give God his due for the things he has done in your life. But as a Worshiper I bow my head and my heart in reverence to the only true God who saves me, who sustains me and is keeping me. And I worship from an attitude of gratitude, not for what I can get from God, but I worship because HE is

God! I worship because I am sick. I am sick of being "stuck on stupid." I am sick because I am sick and tired of being sick and tired. I am sick because I have a disease. It is called the "I can't help it I tis." In other words, I am a sold out fanatic about my Lord. Nothing I have done, will do and am doing will separate me from my Father. Nothing will stop me from serving God. Nothing can knock me off course of acknowledging his holiness and giving him honor and glory. I worship because it is part of my DNA. I am wired that way. His holiness, his righteousness, his purity is in me. And those sacred characteristics gravitate my Spirit to his Spirit. So when I come in God's house I have to fall on my face. I have to bow my head. I have to sing and shout. I have to pray. I have to praise. I have to obey. I have to exclaim his goodness. He deserves it. He creed it before I existed. It is what I do as a worshiper. It's like expecting a bird to crawl or a rabbit to ski. No, that's not what they do. Birds fly. Rabbits hop. People who belong to God, worship Him in Spirit and in truth. Do you?

My worship is not contingent on my purity or holiness or lifestyle. It does not hinge on if I am right relationship with God. My worship is all about my attitude. It's about paying homage to God because he is God. God is looking down from heaven when we worship. And he is looking at your heart. He is looking at your posture. Are you humble? Are you contrite in spirit? Are you transparent? It is about how you feel about the Most High God. Psalm 57:7 says, "my heart is fixed. God my heart is fixed. I will sing and give praise." Praising and singing songs in unison, lifting holy hands, clapping your hands is all good, but worship involves more body language. It involves bowing to the Most High God. It involves falling to your knees, falling on your face; falling in awe of his goodness; his glory, his splendor and his majesty. Don't get me wrong, it is obvious we can't all fall to our knees in worship due to health and physical issues, however we can bow in homage of who God is. I am saying it is about our conduct and character when we're in God's house. Are we holy and humble? God says, "my flesh and my heart fail, but God is the strength of my life and my portion forever." (Psalm 73:26). We can stop right there. But God. He heals the brokenhearted and binds up their wounds. (Psalm 147:3). My own heart cannot thwart my intentions to worship. You see it's all about your attitude towards God. It's what I believe about God is what I'm going to do in worship.

When I think about worship, I think about bible characters from old who worshiped God. The bible says in Mark 7:24-30 the Syrophoenician woman worshiped God. I believe a true worshiper goes beyond being a praiser. They transcend the natural and gain immediate access to the supernatural power of God because of what they believe about him. A worship is undeniably convinced of God's holiness; his power; his wisdom and his ability to do all things—knowing that he can never fail. He cannot change his mind and he cannot die. Is what you believe that enables you to be a true worshiper.

The reason I can say that is because God gave me this revelation. He said, "you don't have to be a true worshiper to praise me, but you must be a true believer to worship me." In other words, we can all praise him, but we can't all worship God unless we believe. We must believe God is who he said he is. God is Jehovah Ralpha. God is our healer. He is Jehovah Rho-hee, he is our shepherd. He is Jehovah Sab-oath, he is the Lord of hosts. He is Jehoavh Nissi, he is the our banner. He is Jehovah Shalom, our peace. He is Jehovah Mekadishki, he is our Sanctifier. The book of John is replete with the word, "believe." John 4:24 says, "true worshipers worship in spirit and in truth." Jesus didn't call for true praisers, he called for true worshipers! Believing in God positions you to be in the right place to be a true worshiper. Believing is the catalyst to create an atmosphere for worship. Believing will transport your mind to the throne room of the Almighty!

True worshipers can praise and worship. They are the ones God seeks. So sinners should catch on fire because of believers acts of worship. What's in the house?

God demands true worship and authentic worship. True worship is like smoke you smell it before you see it. And where there is smoke there's bound to be fire! What does your worship smell like? Worship is not about you. Worship is not for you. Worship is intended for God. The object and focus of worship is God. The bottom line is if we want to see God show up in this house we're going to have to do something.

Let me give you three ways I believe we should worship God.

We should worship:

- Humbly;
- Obediently; and
- Broken

The word of God says Jesus, "humbled himself and became obedient to the grave." If Jesus humbled himself, shouldn't we? God's word says, "I will oppose the proud, but give grace to the humble" (1 Peter 5:5b). And 1 Peter 5:6 says, "humble yourself under the Almighty hand of God and he will lift you up." When we humble ourselves we demonstrate to God our need for him. Secondly, we should come to God's house in obedience. 1 Samuel 15:22 says, "God prefers obedience over sacrifice." Obedience is pleasing God. John 14:23 tells us, "if we love God we will obey his teachings." He also says, "if you obey my commands; you will remain in my love, just as I have obeyed my Father's command and remain in his love." Jesus was obedient. We should be too. Lastly, we should come to God's house broken because the church is a hospital. We all are sick with some type of ailment or imperfection that only God can fix. When we come broken we are admitting we need Jesus to be our heart-fixer, our mind regulator and our heavy-load sharer. The scripture says, "the sacrifices of God are a broken spirit and a contrite heart." (Psalm 51:17). Contrite means to pound to pieces or worn out. Anybody here worn out? If so, you're in the right place for Jesus to fix you. What's in the house? Broken-ness is not inability, but it's assurance in Jesus' sufficiency.

Now that I've told you how you should worship, let me tell you what some hindrances to worship. The bible says true worshipers worship in spirit and truth. I believe the reason why some of us can't worship in spirit and truth is because we have blockages. That's why I'm so mad and disgusted with some of our houses of worship. I'm an environmentalist. As an environmentalist I believe we should make God's house conducive for his presence. We should woooo him that he desires to show up. Our worship should be "flames of fire" for God. Some of us are just wet ashes. And still others have allowed their flame to get snuffed out. That's a blockage and it hinders our worship. Here are some other blockages:

- Mindset
- Unrepented sin
- Unforgiveness
- Anger
- Indecent desires
- Pride
- Time

The list above identifies common distractions we grapple with as Christians. Can you imagine what it most of have been like for the Christians of old? As we go to our text we are going to examine two priests who God had issue with. It was their worship that God had a problem with. But first let me paint you a picture of how the Old Testament believers were sweet a smelling aroma to God's nostrils. Assiduous attention was given to every detail in the sanctuary. It should remind us that God cares about the intricate details of our lives.

Let's look at Leviticus. In chapter 10, verse 1-3 we have the story of two brothers, Abihu and Nadab. They were appointed, anointed, consecrated and ordained by God to serve as priests, but their worship was sinful. It stunk, it was unacceptable. Why? There are several assertions theologians raise as possible answers. 1) is they could have worshipped at the wrong time; 2) the incense they brought to God could have been tainted or they were carless to bring the wrong kind of incense or possibly they were drunk; and 3) a third possible reason is that it could be that they brought their own cisterns with fire already in them; instead of using the fire from the altar of incense. All assertions are plausible reasons that God was not pleased with their worship.

Cisterns are vessels used to burn incense. In a biblical context incense is considered as "praise and prayers" to God. Psalm 141:2 says, "let my prayers be set before you like incense." I believe Nadab and Abihu's sin was that their worship was counterfeit. It was not authentic. It was fake. It was a fraud. They merely went through the motion of worship without having the mindset or heart to worship. Are we guilty of that? Their motives were wrong. Their worship should have been a sweet aroma instead it was a stench, an odor that offended God, which caused him to consume them. That's right. God burned them to a crisp. He did it because their worship was "unholy." Their motive was wrong. What's in the house?

Exodus 30:19-21 says they should have washed their hands and feet. Leviticus 1:2 says they were to offer an animal without defect. Leviticus 5 says they didn't bring the right kind of fire. Many of us go to church Sunday after Sunday without praying, without confessing our sin, or consulting God on what he desires in worship. What kind of fire are you bringing into God's house? Do you have any fire? Is your fire a flickering flame or a towering inferno? Many of us have the nerve to walk in the Lord's house empty—devoid of power and stinky. If fire is in the house you ought to smell something burning. What's in the house?

Fire represents God's holiness in three ways. Fire represents God in 1) judgment—God literally destroyed Sodom and Gomorrah by fire. 2) Fire represents God's manifestation of himself and what he approves. He appeared to Moses in a burning bush; he appeared as a pillar of fire to the Israelites in the wilderness; and 3) Fire represents God's purification—he is a refiner and purifier and he tests the quality of men's work. And he did say that he has a "lake of fire" reserved for those who don't believe. (Rev 20:15). God's fire is like a battery, when you match up a positive post with a positive you get power. But when you match a negative with a positive; there's no power. Are you packing power in the house of God?

That was Abihu and Nadab's issue. They had no power. Their worship was not right. It was not true. And it was not holy. When holiness comes into contact with holiness it should be a fiery combustion. It should strike a chord in your spirit that resonates on the outside. That wasn't the case for these two priests.

So what's acceptable worship? I'm glad you asked. Let me tell you if you want to be a pleasing aroma in God's nostrils you should be offering him four things. In the Old Testament the priest had to offer dead animals to remove their sin before speaking to God. But in the New Testament the believer need only confess his sin and John says, "God is faithful and just to forgive us and cleanse us from unrighteousness. (1 John 1:9). Then we can go to God with unhindered worship. As saints we are to offer God: 1) our body; Romans 12:1 says, "present your body as a living sacrifice holy and pleasing unto him that is our reasonable act of worship." Amen.

As New Testament believers we should offer our bodies to God. Our bodies don't belong to us anymore, but to him. Our bodies are where the Holy Spirit resides. Why would you defile his house? But many of us do it everyday by what we drink, eat or even what we smoke.

Secondly, we are to give God our praise. The bible says, "let everything that has breath praise the Lord." (Psalm 75:6). What does your praise smell like? Is it a sweet smelling aroma? Or is air pollution? Remember we can all praise God, but we can't all worship God—unless we are a believer.

Thirdly, we are to give God our substance, which means our finances, our treasure—that which God has so graciously bestowed upon us. We are to give a portion back to honor him. Malachi 3:10 says, "bring all the tithe into the storehouse." That doesn't mean a tip. A tithe is a tenth of your earnings.

And finally, as N.T. believers we are to worship God with our service. Colossians 3:23-24 says, in "whatever you do work as it with all your heart, as working for the Lord. Not for men, since you know that you will receive an inheritance from the Lord as a reward. It is the Lord you are serving." When we serve god whether in the church or in the world; we should be a sweet smelling aroma to those we come into contact. So now we know what is acceptable worship. We should do better. What's in the house?

God says you cannot approach him any kind of way. Why? We sin because man has a propensity and a proclivity to sin. It is our nature. That is why we must confess our sins. We must cleanse our mind and heart from the dirt of the world. We must consecrate our body and our mind for service so that we can commune with the Master in a way that pleases him. God wants to devour those dead things in our life. He desires to rekindle the fire he put in you. As we go to God with sincerity and purity of heart we should be compelled to worship him with every part of our body.

In particular, we should worship with our hands, our ears and our feet. Aaron and his sons washed their hands and feet whenever they entered the Tent of Meeting or approached the altar. We can learn a lesson from these witnesses and do likewise. In these examples we can also identify the rewards of worship.

Let's hear from the Syrophoenician woman in Mark 7:24-30. She had a demon-possessed daughter. The bible says when she heard Jesus was coming she fell at his feet worshiping. God delivered her daughter because she worshipped. That was her reward.

The bible says in Mark 5:22 when Jairus the synagogue leader's son was sick, he demonstrated what he believed by falling to his feet in worship. God cured Jairus' son because he worshiped. That was his reward for worship.

The bible says in John 11:32 that when Mary heard Jesus was coming by after her brother Lazarus was dead she executed her faith in God and fell at his feet in worship. And God rewarded Mary's worship by resurrecting Lazarus from the dead.

The bible says in Matthew 8:22 when the leper heard Jesus was coming he expressed his worship by kneeling to his feet in worship. And God healed his body because he worshiped. That was his reward.

The bible says in John 9:38 when the blind man expressed his confession of faith he worshiped. As a result God restored his sight because he worshiped. That was his reward.

Finally, when John the Revelator was taken up by the Spirit the bible says in Revelations 1:17 that he expressed what he believed by falling at Jesus' feet in worship. And God showed him a new heaven and a new earth because he worshiped. That was his reward.

When we worship God in spirit and in truth we compel God to act. And we can examine the results. Imagine what he will do for you when you truly worship him in spirit and truth? What's in the house? Remember our destination is purification then perfection.

He wants you to come humbly, obediently and broken.

Aaron and his sons set the standard for us. It is the anointing of the priesthood that will continue to all generations. (Exo 40:15). We must come to God's house with the intent to worship. When we do, God's shekinah glory will show up. Bring your power and God's power and see a towering inferno of praise.

I am convinced when we truly worship in spirit and in truth God will bless us. I don't know about you, but when I'm all by myself that is when my worship is pure. My worship is unadulterated, unhindered. My worship is unashamed, uninterrupted and uncontained. I get the "I can't help it I tis"! I have to lift my hands. I have to bow down. I have to run. I have to stand to my feet. I have to raise my praise. I have to dance. I have to shout. I don't mind turning God's house out—because I am a true worshiper. I don't know about you, but when I come into God's house I have to let him know how much I love him. I have to let him know how much I adore him, how much I exalt him, and how much I want to be like him. Is there anybody here who came to worship God?

Corporately we can worship God. Individually we can worship God, but when we get on one accord worshiping God it arrests God's attention. It compels him to rest, bless and manifest his glory in his house. Are there any true worshipers in the house? Holler if you hear me!

When the World is Crumbling, Just have Faith

*H*earing the topic of this bible study shouldn't frighten you. After all we realize that we aren't of the world. We are in the world, but not of it. We're just pilgrims passing through. This place is not our home. Today we want to talk about faith. We will answer three questions. 1) What is faith? 2) Where do you get faith? And 3) How do we activate our faith?

We all know what faith is right? Faith is the substance of things hoped for; the evidence of things not seen. But what does that mean? I like to offer another definition of faith. Faith is believing and receiving what God has revealed. It can b defined as trust in God or trust in Jesus Christ. This trust compels you to a loving relationship. It produces good work. For God says, "now these three remain: faith, hope and love. But the greatest of these is love." We as Christians know that our faith is our glue that holds us together. It is said that only what you do for Christ will last. And 1 Corinthians 13:13 teaches us that only love will count. Just as "faith" without works is dead, "works" without love is dead. People are pleased with desirable acts, but God is pleased by acts of faith and love.

Let's answer the question, where did we get faith? My bible tells me in Romans 10:17, "faith comes from hearing and hearing by the word of God." So that tells me "faith" can only be activated when the word of God is spoken. Don't miss that key word, "hear." I can't "hear" the word of God by reading it to myself. I can't "hear" the word of God by believing it in my heart. I can't "hear" the word by thinking it in my mind. I have to speak it out of my mouth. You have to say it out loud right? Or someone has to speak it, teach it or preach it to you right? So for me to activate my faith I have to audibly speak out of my mouth what I am trusting God to do. I get my faith from God. I ask him into my heart. It is with my heart that I believe. It is with my mouth that I confess that I believe in Jesus. (Romans 10:9). So it is safe to say that I get my faith from my Father.

Romans 4:17 says, "as it is written: I have made you a father of many nations. He is our Father in the sight of God, in whom he believed—the God who gives life to dead and calls things that are not as though they were." That sounds like faith to me—what about you? Faith is calling something you desire to have even though you can't see it yet. Faith is acting on what you believe you heard from God. It is believing and receiving what God has revealed. Doing what you hear the Spirit of the Lord say to you is activating your faith.

Hebrews 11 speaks about four men who were heroes of faith: Abel, Enoch, Noah and Abraham. Let's review their example and see what we can glean from these scriptures. It's important to note the word "faith" is mentioned 11 times in the first 10 verses of Hebrews eleven. First, let's look at verse

3, it says, "by faith we understand the universe was formed at God's command." Genesis 1:1 says, "in the beginning God created the heavens and the earth." And John 1:1 says, "in the beginning was the Word, and the Word was with God and the Word was God. He was with God in the beginning." Who is he? He is Jesus Christ. Heaven and earth "heard" the Word speak to the world so it had to form. Remember faith comes by hearing and hearing by the Word of God. Therefore, we believe God formed the world by faith!

By faith, Abel gave God a better sacrifice than his brother Cain. According to the Word (Gen 4:3-5) Abel was credited for being a righteous man. Cain's sacrifice was fruit from the ground, while Abel's was fat from the flock. You could look at it like Cain gave God a tip while Abel gave God a tithe. Abel's offering was more substantial. It was better. Verse 4b states, "and the Lord had respect unto Abel and to his offering." Cain gave to get credit for himself. Abel gave to obey God's will. The difference was Abel gave his sacrifice by faith. Because of that he is one of the one "heroes of faith."

By Faith, at the tender age of 65 Enoch became the Father of Methuselah. And after that the bible says, "he walked with God 300 years and had other sons and daughters." (Gen 5:22). All together Enoch lived 365 years then he was taken away. He was taken away from this life so that he wouldn't experience death. Now, he is one our "heroes of faith." The scripture says, "by faith" he was taken away! Wouldn't you love to have that testimony?

When your world is crumbling down—you need to have some faith! Things are never what they appear. If the enemy can distract you from your destiny—he will do it! We've got to learn how to take distress, destruction and the dirt the devil deals us and turn it into our good. The bible says in Genesis 50:22, you "meant to harm, but God intended it for my good." We can turn our situation around if we just apply a little faith. All you need is mustard seed size. So stop fretting over stuff you can't control anyway. We need to drop four inches from the floor and realize we're stronger on our knees than we can ever be on our feet.

Our third patriarch of faith is Noah. You know Noah right? The bible says, "Noah was a righteous man, blameless among the people and he walked with God." (Gen 6:9). By faith, Noah believed what he heard from God. When God told him that he was going to destroy al the people and the earth; Noah took God at his word. And he trusted his own ability to make an "ark"—something he had never seen before or knew how to make. Because of that God established his covenant with Noah and his family. Noah's obedience earned him the right to be called a patriarch of faith.

Do you have that type of blind faith to trust God in all situations? I'm telling you the faith that can move mountains gets God's attention. The bible says, "show me your faith without deeds, and I will show you my faith by what I do." (James 4:18b). In other words, some of us think we can get by—by just saying, "I'm believing God for a miracle and don't ever do anything to back up with at we believe. That's crazy!

Action is a requirement for faith to work. So what are you going to do when your world is crumbling? Are you going to have a pity party? Or are you going to pray in faith and speak to your situation in the name of Jesus and call those things be not as they were? I'm just asking about faith.

There's a story told about a little boy. He always heard his grandmother say, "I'm standing on faith." One day the apartment where the little boy lived caught on fire and he couldn't get out. He went to the window, but his small legs weren't tall enough to get out. So he ran to the room and grabbed a book to stand on to get out. It didn't work. So the little boy got several more books to help him get out of the window. They were all too small. Finally, he ran to his grandmother's room and got her bible. He got out of the window by standing on her bible. When he was reunited with his family, they asked him, "how did you get out?" The little boy said, "I always heard grandmother say she was standing on faith. And I remember her holding her bible when she said it, so I grabbed it and stood on it to get out of the window." This is a lesson we can take to heart. And that's the kind of faith we need today. If we're going to make it in this world; we have to stand on our faith.

Our final "hero of faith" is Abraham. We all know Abraham, right? When God spoke to Abraham he was not "Abraham." As a matter of fact his name was "Abram." (Gen 12:1-4). We read in the word that Abram heard God's voice and obeyed. God told him to go to a country that he had never been to before and leave everything behind. Abram was 75 years old at the time. He took his wife, Sarai, his nephew Lot and people he had acquired in Hara. He went by "faith" and God gave him four personal promises. First, he told Abram: 1) I will make you into a great nation; 2) I will bless you—which was two-fold meaning God would bless him temporarily and spiritually; 3) God will make his name great; and 4) Abram would be a channel of blessings. (Gen 12:2). Meaning he would be a lender never a borrower as it states in Deuteronomy 12:6.

The final promises God gave were to Abraham and the Gentile people. He said: 1) I will bless you; 2) whoever curses you, I will curse and 3) all people on earth will be blessed by you. (Gen 12:3). Abram was an heir of God's promises and he became a "hero of faith" because of his obedience to take God at his word.

In our study we can see that faith is believing and receiving what God has revealed. We see that faith comes by hearing and hearing by the Word of God. And we see that faith is activated when we hear God's voice through his Word. What I love about faith is that it doesn't come by osmosis. In other words, I can't get it by wishing it or blinking my eyes three times and turning in a circle. I have to believe in my heart and speak it from my mouth; then act on what I say I believe. It's like a math formula. I think it's called the Pythagorean theory. It simply says, "if this then that." For faith to work in your life you have to have "trust" in God. So you could say, "if you trust in God and do what he says than you can conquer anything in life." That's faith in action.

Another thing I love about faith is what God says in his Word. In Romans 4:18, it says, "against all hope Abraham in hope believed and so became the father of many nations, just as it had been said to him, so shall your offspring be. Without weakening in faith, he faced the fact that his body was a good as dead—since he was about a hundred years old—and that Sarah's womb was also dead. Yet, he did not waver through unbelief regarding the promise of God, but he was strengthened in his faith and gave glory to God, being fully persuaded that God had power to do what he had promised." That's amazing faith! We have that same promise from God. "We can do all things through Christ who strengthens us." (Phil 4:13). If you want to be strong in your faith—trust God and take him at his Word.

The best part of faith is that it only takes a little bit. Chapter 5 in Romans says, "therefore since we have been justified through faith, we have peace with God through our Lord Jesus Christ." That's shouting news! We have peace with God because of our faith. So, when your world is crumbling down—you can have peace because you have faith in God. Praise Jesus!

He is our peace-maker. He is our company keeper. He is our way maker. And he is our will in the middle of a will. There's no one like our God. He is the alpha and omega. The rose of Sharon; the bright and morning star. Nothing can separate us from the love of God—not my past, or my future and not even me. I don't know about you, but I' going to keep the faith and keep running the race. I will always remember that Jesus has me in the palm of his hands and nothing can snatch me out of them. The bible says, "fight the good fight of faith." (1 Tim 6:12). I think I will. Remember we are more than conquerors and we can win if we choose to have faith.

Woman, Know Who You Are

$\mathscr{P}$salm 139:13-14 states we are "fearfully and wonderfully made." I am going to talk about three things in this text. I am going to talk about the: 1) **intimacy** of our relationship with God, (v. 1-4). 2) the **inescapable** presence of God (v. 7-12); and 3) the **identity** of God's creation (v. 13-16).

Verse 1 through 4 ought to strike a chord in your heart. It ought to cause you to shrink in shame. It ought to make you stand bold to proclaim His greatness. Intimacy with the Master is living out your purpose. You can only live out your purpose when God shows you "why" he created you! Many of us are not interested in the "why"—we're too busy jumping and shouting on "what" God has done—losing sight on "why." "Why" is operating in your purpose. It's acting out what God created you to be perform in the earth. It is your destiny. You are no threat to the devil in the "what" of your life. You are more dangerous to the devil when you begin to operate in the "why" of who you are! As woman of God you need to know God has a plan for your life.

Verse five states, "you hem me in—before and behind—that is protection. That's why we can do any and everything to our bodies with other people. That's why we can say anything because we don't understand "who" we are and "whose" we are. If we did we wouldn't be doing it. David said in this Psalm God is a all-knowing; all-seeing and all-wise God. He knows what we're going to do before we do it. He knows what we're going to say before we say it. He knows where we're going before we go. He knows when he's going to wake us up and when he's going to put us asleep.

Verse six states, "such knowledge is too wonderful or lofty for us to understand." In other words, the Psalmist is stating God cannot be figured out like a puzzle or played like a game. He is the God of the universe. He is the Sovereign Lord and King. The prophet Isaiah said "there's no searching of his understanding." His thoughts are higher than our thoughts; his ways are higher than our ways." Who can fathom them? That is because He wants you to trust Him and believe in Him. The understanding will come as you develop a deeper relationship with the Father. This knowledge God has about me is too wonderful. I can't conceive it. I am not able to understand the depth, the width and the span of intimacy of our relationship. It is like knowing how to do Chinese algebra—it's too hard. I just need to know that He knows me. God is well acquainted with his creation.

The second thing I want to share is the inescapable presence of God.

Verse seven begins with a series of questions about where can I go from God's presence. Look at it. Do you see it? Each preceding verse begins with "if."

If I go to the heavens;

If I make my bed;

If I rise on the wings of the dawn;

If I settle on the side of the sea;

Then verse ten interrupts and answers the four questions by stating "even" there your hand will guide me. Your right hand will hold me fast. Anybody knows what it feels like for God's hand to be on you? Verse 11 begins with a question, "if" I say, "surely the darkness will cover (hide) me and light become night. In other words, David is saying when I plot evil in my mind, I think I'm getting away with it because I think you can't see me at night when I'm doing my creeping and crawling. I think you can't see me slipping and dipping. I think you can't see me sliding and hiding, but before David can finish his thought he realizes in verse 12 "even the darkness will not be dark for you." David says "the night will shine like the day." In other words, all your knaving, slipping and sliding will be exposed to the Father. Why? It is because verse 12 says "darkness is light to you."

You have to remember from the beginning of time when God stepped out into nothing and made something He commanded the darkness to become light. Remember Genesis 1:2 he said, "darkness was over the surface of the deep and the Spirit of God was hovering over the waters." Verse 3 states, "God said, "let there be light." Verse 4 states, "he separated the light from the darkness." That tells me whatever I'm doing that If I have to tell myself, "the darkness will cover me"—then I know it's not any good. Hebrews 4:13 states, "nothing is hidden from God."

So why do we think we can escape the inescapable presence of God? I want you to think about it.

Now we're going to go deeper. We've talked about the intimacy of our relationship with our Father. And we talked about the inescapable presence of our Father; now we are going to talk about the identity of God's creation.

Verse 13 exclaims and proclaims we are the result of God's personal handiwork! He created your inner man to have communion with Him. Where God resides Jesus always abides. He gave you life. Your life is in Him. Then he placed you in your mother's womb. We really have to get a concept of "who we are." He says he created your inmost being. Remember when God created man? He took the dust of the earth and blew breath into man's nostrils and he became a living being.

Look at it. God took you (woman) out of a man. You have his breath in your being. Then he fashioned, formed and designed your outer appearance to reflect the inner image of Him. Do you need a moment? He did it in the person of a woman— whom he created to be the life-giver; the producer of life; the incubator of life. So in essence He took you out of man. He placed you in a woman so that you could praise the Son of Man who made you! WOW! Do you really know who you are?

That is why we can praise God. We are fearfully and wonderfully made. Fearfully is reverence for God. Wonderfully made means it can't be duplicated or replicated by man. There is no cloning here. You were supernaturally created by God's own hand. That is too wonderful! Who else but God can do that? But maybe that's too lofty for you to understand. All I know is that no child of the King of Kings should have a low self-esteem. And I will tell you why. Look at the following scriptures:

- Isaiah 43:7 says, "everyone who is called by my name; . . . . I created for my glory."
- Jeremiah 1:5 says, "I (God) formed you. I knew you before you were born. I set you apart."
- Genesis 1:27 says, "God created man in his own image."
- Genesis 5:1-2 "God created man. He made him in the likeness of God. He blessed them."
- Hebrews 2:11 says, "Both the one who makes men holy and those who are made holy are the same family."
- 1 Peter 3:3-4 says, "your beauty, should not come from outside adornment; it should be inner beauty of a gentle and quiet spirit."
- 1 Peter 2:9-10 says, we are "a chosen people, a holy nation, a royal priesthood which is of great worth in God's sight."
- 1 Peter 1:15-16 says, "be holy in all you do. It is written be holy because I am holy."
- 2 Corinthians 5:17 says, "if you're in Christ . . . you are a new creature; old is gone and new has come."
- 1 John 4:9-10 says, "this is how God showed his love. He sent his only Son, that we might live through him."

That's why you can praise him. You can see that in Psalm 139, verse 13-16 talks about what God has done in the past. Verse 14 talks about why I praise God in the present. And we know that we can praise God for what he has done in our past. We can praise God for what He is doing right now. But I double dog dare you to praise God for what he is going to do in your future. You ought to thank God for what he's doing right now because he is sovereign. Isaiah 45:11-12 states, he created all mankind. Isaiah 43:21 states, he formed us to proclaim his praises. Isaiah 52:7 states, how beautiful are the feet of those who proclaim peace and salvation. Are you proclaiming anything about God today?

Isaiah 43:4 says, "you're precious and honored in his sight." He loves you. That's why we ought to praise God.

Isaiah 43:7 says, "he created you for his glory." That's why we ought to praise God.

Psalms 22:9 says, "he brought you out of your mother's womb and made you trust in him; even at your mother's breast." Verse 10 says, "from birth I was cast upon you—from my mother's womb you have seen my God."

Job said, "I will live because I have God's breath in my nostrils." So do you . . . will you praise Him?

Job 33:4 says, "The Spirit of God has made me, the breath of the Almighty has given me life."

Verse 15 in Psalm 139 says your frame was not hidden from your Creator. Your relationship with him is so special that he had to perform and perfect your beginning; your conception; and your existence in a high secure place. This speaks to your unique position in God. He had to make sure that there were no breaches in security. He made sure there was no outside interference; no outside disturbances. So he took a speck of dust and fashioned you in the earth next to your man. Your frame is sewn up in God. Don't get it twisted. The Lord has you in his grip.

Verse 16 in Psalm 139 says, "your eyes saw my unformed body." You need to know you were on God's mind before you came into being. He thought about how you should look before he created you. He took the time to determine the intricate details of your being. (your smile, skin color, how you would hold you head, the nuisances of your personality; your features and your ways, etc.). God has you in the precious palm of his hands. He will keep you together. There is no since fretting over the small stuff. Your Daddy has your back, front and everything else in between.

God determined your beginning and your end before any of it came into existence. He said, "all your days are written in his book." It was predestined for you to be here baby. Your name is written right next to his name. (Revelation 21:27). HALLELUJAH! That means he knows you without equivocation. He knows you undoubtedly. And he knows without hesitation or second thought that you belong to him. Your intimacy with Jesus is predicated on his relationship with his father. It's that type of relationship that the Father and Son share. He shares with us when we invite him in.

Psalms 50:2 says, "God is perfect in beauty." So are you! You came from him and because he is in you; your beauty shines through.

Remember God cares for you. He loves you. Don't forget God know whose you are. You are intimately connected to God. Your presence cannot be breached. Therefore God's presence is inescapable in your life. And finally your identity is being a child of the King of Kings! Somebody say, 'AMEN!'